A Decade of Niger

A Decade of Niger

Politics, Economy and Society 2008–2017

By

Klaas van Walraven

BRILL

LEIDEN | BOSTON

The Library of Congress Cataloging-in-Publication Data is available online at
http://catalog.loc.gov

Typeface for the Latin, Greek, and Cyrillic scripts: "Brill". See and download: brill.com
/brill-typeface.

ISBN 978-90-04-40141-9 (paperback)
ISBN 978-90-04-40144-0 (e-book)

Contents

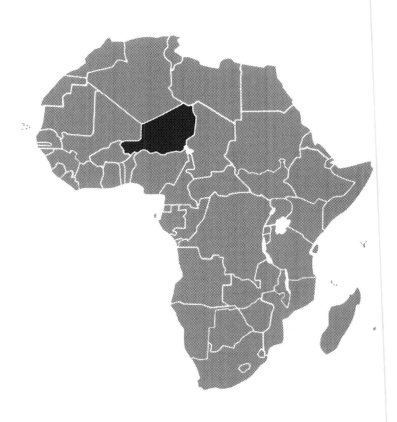

Niger in 2008

The Tuareg rebellion continued, though at a low level of intensity. Casualties mounted among civilians, who fell victim to army brutality, landmines and rebel abductions. The rebels gained an important new supporter but also experienced their first split. At year's end, the military situation was inconclusive. The simmering tension between President Tandja and former Prime Minister Hama Amadou developed into open hostility, with the latter being detained on embezzlement charges. Media suffered attacks and harassment, especially from the government, which also banned humanitarian operations by 'Médecins Sans Frontières' (MSF). Cereal harvests were fairly good, thanks to abundant rains. Social tension was limited, despite increasing food and fuel prices. Uranium prices were renegotiated, leading to higher state revenues. The government was ordered by the ECOWAS court of justice to pay compensation to a victim of slavery.

Domestic Politics

The *armed rebellion* initiated in 2007 by the Tuareg-led 'Mouvement des Nigériens pour la Justice' (MJN) continued unabated. On 8 January, the director of a private radio station was killed after driving over a landmine planted in a suburb of the capital Niamey. The explosion occurred in the Yantala district, home to many army officers. The MJN denied responsibility, which came after similar explosions in other cities. Government officials spoke of "urban terrorism" and called for the formation of vigilante committees. The incident marked the extension of the rebellion from its strongholds in the northern desert regions to settled parts of the country and showed that the MJN had supporters in urban areas, probably among Tuaregs living there.

© KONINKLIJKE BRILL NV, LEIDEN, 2019 | DOI:10.1163/9789004401440_002

On 22 January, rebels abducted 11 people in the city of Tanout in Niger's east, including the local prefect and a security official. Seven soldiers were killed in the attack, according to the MJN. The government reported three deaths and five wounded. Three days later, five civilians were kidnapped near the uranium mining town of Arlit in the north, including a teacher (teachers in Niger are regarded as representatives of the state). The probable target was the deputy head of Niger's human rights commission, who had been expected to travel to the area but had cancelled his visit. The *kidnapping of civilians*, like the indiscriminate planting of landmines, led to calls from AI to respect the Geneva conventions, which ban the taking of civilian hostages. Twenty-five of these, including the prefect of Tanout, were released on 10 March to mark the uprising's first anniversary.

In mid-March, rebels launched an attack on a military base at Bani Bangou near the Malian border. Three soldiers were reportedly killed and one captured. The government responded to the continued offensive, as it had the previous year, with a combination of denial as to the nature of the uprising and harsh *retaliatory action*, usually targeting civilians. Arguing that its opponents had no political objectives but were bandits and traffickers, the regime persisted in its refusal to negotiate. An AI report published on 3 April claimed that the army had killed, tortured and abducted several civilians in reprisal for the deaths of five soldiers during operations in the mountains around Agadez, the northern capital, at the end of March. Civilians were allegedly forced to drive ahead of a military convoy to detonate landmines. At least eight civilians were said to have been arbitrarily executed, while some were also tortured. On 30 March, four inhabitants of a village were detained by soldiers and subsequently disappeared. The government denied the assertions (as was its habit with most NGO reports), claiming it had killed ten bandit-smugglers in an offensive in which five of its own soldiers had been killed. On 19 April, the National Assembly adopted an anti-terror law targeting the possession of explosives, hostage-taking, attacks on transport and unlawful possession of radioactive materials.

Renewed hostilities erupted at the end of May, when the government claimed it had killed 11 insurgents in the Agadez area, which the MJN asserted was an attack on a nomad camp near Iferouâne, the town further north where the uprising had started the previous year. The rebels claimed that there were seven casualties and that they were civilians. On 14 May, they succeeded in kidnapping the vice chairman of Niger's human rights commission in Tanout, engaged in peace initiatives in the area, together with his nephew. They were released ten days later. The pattern repeated itself when on 22 June four French employees of an Areva-owned uranium mine were seized in Arlit, only to be released three days later. As with many of these attacks, this one was calculated to humiliate the government, which had pledged to provide protection to mining companies. Though at a low level of intensity, the hostilities led to mounting casualties. Around 30 government soldiers were missing (taken hostage) at the start of the year. By mid-year some 70 had reportedly been killed since the beginning of the uprising. *Casualties* on the MJN side were believed to be at least 200, one of whom was the movement's deputy commander. This did not prevent a mortar attack on the city of Agadez on 10 July.

The MJN's position was potentially strengthened when on 31 January Rhissa Ag Boula announced his support for the rebel cause. Ag Boula, a Tuareg leader who had represented the rebels in the 1995 peace negotiations that ended a previous rebellion, had been sought out by President Mamadou Tandja in 2006 to persuade Tuareg leaders to preserve the 1995 accord. Earlier in 2004–05 he had been sacked as minister of tourism and jailed for complicity in the murder of a member of the government party, 'Mouvement National pour la Société du Développement' (MNSD). Ag Boula criticised the government for its refusal to engage in dialogue and for issuing licences for uranium prospecting and warned that the MJN would attack mining company operations. His *defection* to the rebels meant the loss of his moderating influence on the Tuareg community, while his international reputation made it harder to pretend that the MJN was nothing more than a bandit movement.

In July, MJN chief Aghaly Ag Alambo demanded that government and mining firms set aside 20%–30% of uranium earnings for the benefit of the local population. This was actually a concession compared to previous demands. By that time, the MJN had suffered its first *split* – a recurrent feature of Tuareg movements. On 30 May, several leading MJN members formed a new group, the 'Front des Forces de Redressement' (FFR), accusing the MJN of lacking a political strategy and of being ineffective in the fight against government troops. The new group, which included the political itinerant Ag Boula, as well as the former MJN spokesperson, also condemned the MJN's use of landmines. The potential weakening of the rebel cause was highlighted by government statements in June that around 500 combatants had laid down their arms. A statement to this effect was broadcast by the government in August, but the MJN claimed these were rebel allies in Mali, not those fighting the government in Niamey. Nevertheless, several MJN members did lay down their arms – some in a ceremony in Zinder in August during which a government official stepped on a landmine setting off a chain reaction that killed one and injured dozens of others.

Two months of relative quiet came to an end with a *renewed outbreak* of violence in October. The Toubou-led 'Front des Forces Armées Révolutionnaires du Sahara' (FARS), which had also risen up against the Niamey government during the 1990s, had by then also become active again. In April, it joined forces with the MJN and claimed to have killed seven government soldiers and abducted six. The government, which confirmed the clashes, claimed two people had died, one on each side. At year's end, the Canadian Robert Fowler, appointed as the UN secretary general's *special envoy* to Niger, went missing. He was apparently kidnapped together with a fellow Canadian just 45 km outside Niamey (14 December). While UN officials said he was travelling on official business, the government claimed he was in Niger on a private visit, a claim that underscored the sensitive nature of his mission and mandate, since the Niamey authorities refuse any UN mediation. At first, spokesmen for the FFR claimed responsibility for the abduction but later retracted the claim, leaving Fowler's whereabouts and the responsibility for his disappearance shrouded in mystery.

The rivalry of previous years between President Tandja and ex-Prime Minister Hama Amadou, both MNSD stalwarts, came to a head in June. Replaced as prime minister in May 2007 for his response to a corruption scandal in which two of his former ministers were implicated, Amadou was now himself accused by the National Assembly of misappropriating funds to the value of € 152,500. Several MNSD members voted with the opposition to press charges, and although the affair was unrelated to the embezzlement scandal that rocked the education and health ministries in 2006, the former prime minister was imprisoned on 26 June. The *ex-premier's detention* was politically explosive as Amadou had already announced his candidature for the next presidential elections. Since Amadou continued as MNSD chair and it had been rumoured for years that Tandja, though constitutionally barred from seeking re-election, might wish to stand for a third term, there was a clear political motive behind Amadou's arrest.

This was confirmed on 31 July by the dismissal of two of Amadou's confidants, his former cabinet chief Amadou Sala and an advisor, Hamidou Tchiana. This was the climax of a *purge* in the preceding weeks during which a dozen of Amadou's collaborators had been stripped of their positions. Amadou supporters demonstrating at the behest of their leader were dispersed by police. With the majority of MNSD members remaining loyal to him and accusing Tandja of a witch hunt, another demonstration took place on 20 October. Party sections in Tillabéri and Zinder reputedly tried to remove Amadou from the MNSD chairmanship. Consequently, the ruling party faced growing *internal fissures*. Suspicions proliferated that Tandja wished to prevent Hama Amadou from standing for president. It was speculated that Tandja would groom his inexperienced son Ousmane, trade attaché in Beijing, for the position. Earlier rumours that the president might attempt to change the constitution to enable him to stand for a third term also gathered momentum. On 31 October, his supporters staged a rally in Zinder calling for his continuance in office.

Thus, the next presidential polls, scheduled for December 2009, not only cast a long shadow but also exposed the ferocity with which politicians treated each other, potentially jeopardising the long-term stability of the political system. This threat was also evident in the treatment of the *media*. The government in August imposed a one-month ban on the Dounia TV and radio group after it had covered the suppression of a pro-Amadou demonstration. Moussa Kaka, reporter of 'Radio France Internationale' (RFI) and chief of the Sarrounia private radio station continued to be held in detention. He had been arrested on 26 September 2007 after telephone conversations with MJN leaders and charged with conspiracy against state authority, and the regime's refusal to back down in the case led to a battle of wills with the courts and international pressure groups. Kaka's reporting of MJN attacks exposed the regime's fragility, thereby humiliating the military and the president, himself a former soldier. In addition, as a RFI reporter Kaka's case appeared to be tied up with the state of French-Nigérien relations, which had cooled the previous year over the renegotiation of the purchase price paid by French nuclear giant Areva for Niger's 'yellow cake'. On 12 February, the court of appeal in Niamey overturned an earlier court decision that phone tap evidence on Kaka was inadmissible. Later, RFI's FM transmissions were suspended for three months, the second ban in a year. The government had already postponed the introduction of new press laws, decriminalising defamation or false news. On 23 June, a senior judge ordered Kaka's release, dismissing charges of collaboration with MJN rebels. However, the public prosecutor appealed, to the fury of the union of private sector journalists, who accused the government of *media harassment*.

In September, the court of appeal reduced the charges, releasing Kaka on 7 October. His release came after mediation by the French government as well as RFI, which, having resumed broadcasting, discontinued high profile reporting. As the courts had never accepted Kaka's defence that his action was part of normal journalistic practice and his release was provisional with the case still pending, the outcome was unsatisfactory for *media freedom*, now threatened by self-censorship. The upcoming 2009 elections, however, may have encouraged the regime to temporarily curb its responses. In the meantime, two French journalists working for European TV station Arte and arrested on 17 December 2007 for filming MJN men in the northern region (banned to the public), had been released after the exertion of international pressure (18 January). Manzo Diallo of Aïr Info, in jail since 9 October 2007, was released conditionally in February.

Relations with international *humanitarian NGOs*, bedevilled since 2005 by the publicity over the famine stalking the countryside that year, took a turn for the worse. On 18 July, MSF had to halt operations in the Maradi region, where it was providing treatment to children suffering from malnutrition. Though Maradi was nowhere near the conflict zone, Nigérien media broadcast the accusation that MSF was aiding the rebellion. As in 2005, the decision led to an undignified dispute about the reality of *malnutrition*, with the government claiming that MSF – which in the past had not always manoeuvred with tact – was exaggerating the problem. The decision apparently emanated from the highest level and an appeal to Tandja to reconsider the situation met with silence. An embarrassed health minister unconvincingly asserted that Niger could handle malnutrition itself. Though there was no famine in 2008, malnutrition is a fact of Sahelian life, notably during the lean months ahead of the autumn harvests. An estimated 14,000 children were said to be at risk and Maradi MPs pleaded that MSF be allowed to continue its relief work.

Foreign Affairs

Relations with *France*, Niger's principal bilateral trading partner and donor, improved after the previous year's renegotiation of the uranium purchase price, which took place against the backdrop of accusations that Areva was aiding the rebellion and the expulsion of its local French director.

The conduct of foreign affairs was principally affected by the repercussions of the rebellion. ECOWAS at the beginning of the year discussed the need for a conference on the sub-regional implications. The Tuareg uprising in neighbouring *Mali* became more intertwined with that of their brethren in Niger. In March, it was rumoured that Malian soldiers, abducted by rebels, had been taken to Niger, following an alliance six months earlier between the MJN and those fighting in northeastern Mali. With the common border running through desert and arid Sahelian zones, which form no barrier to nomads and rebels alike, Mali claimed MJN rebels were fighting alongside Malian Tuaregs. Security experts suspected that both groups cooperated informally. Mali signed an accord with Niamey on security cooperation and in November their foreign ministers met colleagues from Libya, Algeria and Chad in Bamako to discuss a plan of action.

The conflict between the Tuaregs and Mali's government became the subject of Algerian mediation, leading to a ceasefire and the release of hostages mid-year, and Tuareg delegates from Niger also travelled to Algiers for talks earlier on. *Libya*, however, was more active in dealing with the Niger dimension of the Tuareg rebellion. The release of hostages, including the prefect of Tanout, on 10 March was facilitated by the Libyans. President Kadhafi held talks with MJN leader Alambo in southern Libya in August and urged an end to the fighting in both Niger and Mali. All this occurred after some cooling of relations the previous year, when Niger accused Libya – which has a long-standing frontier dispute in Niger's northeast, known to have possible oil reserves – of involvement on MJN's side. On 2 May, however, the prime ministers of both countries met in Niamey to sign deals worth € 100 m for the building of a trans-Saharan highway, an irrigation project and Niger's shoe and textile manufacturing, severely hit by cheap Chinese imports. Other accords dealt with trade and air links.

The *UN* continued to limit its involvement in view of the government's refusal to negotiate with the rebels. UN High Commissioner for Human Rights Louise Arbour called on 23 May for the release of the vice chairman of Niger's human rights commission, kidnapped by the MJN ten days earlier. Later in the year, the world body secured the appointment of Robert Fowler as the secretary general's special envoy. The government could not prevent his abduction in December.

President Tandja, in his capacity as chairman of the summit of the 'Autorité du Bassin du Niger', chaired a joined conference with CEN-SAD in Niamey on 30 April.

Socioeconomic Developments

In contrast with other sub-Saharan countries, there was *little social unrest* as a result of the rise in food and fuel prices. This was the result of the subsidised sale of staple foods and the temporary suspension of taxes and import duties on rice (a staple for the urban population) in March. Fuel prices were kept under control from the beginning of the year. Since government arrears in the payment of student grants and civil servants' salaries – one of the factors in the widespread social unrest in 2005–06 – had been cleared, the quiet on the social front was more or less maintained.

Nevertheless, by February *cereal prices* had risen more than 5% in one month, reaching a level some 12% higher than in the same period the previous year. Localised underproduction, trader speculation and falling imports from neighbouring countries played a role. By May, prices were more than 28% higher than a year before, although this also reflected the usual rises during the lean period. In June, when overall prices rose by 2.6% in a month, the year-on-year *inflation rate* reached more than 10%. In August, it had crept up to 15.4%, the highest in a decade. Predominantly pushed by food and fuel prices, inflation began to come down in the next couple of months with the crash in the oil price and abundant harvests. Yet average consumer price inflation was expected to reach at least 10% for 2008, as compared to 0.1% in 2007.

GDP *growth* was nevertheless expected to hover around the 5–6% mark. This reflected the fact that 30% of GDP is made up by agriculture, which saw above average harvests as a result of abundant *rains*. Partly because of damaging floods, some areas in the south were threatened by moderate food insecurity, in contrast to the north, which, according to the Famine Early Warning Systems Network, faced high *food insecurity*.

After a donor conference in December 2007 came up with $ 236 m in funding, longstanding plans for the construction of the Kandadji *dam* on the Niger river northwest of Niamey, came closer to fruition. A round table of donors and representatives of ABN member states was held in Niamey on 23 June, delivering aid pledges of more than € 900 m. The dam aims to regulate water for irrigation and generate electricity to cope with increasing demand for power and supply problems in Nigeria – at 85%, Niger's principal supplier of electricity. In addition, a deal was signed with China for the transfer of several electrical power units to cope with growing blackouts, caused by ageing *infrastructure*. The Chinese deal could increase power in the capital by 30%. France Télécom won a tender for a fixed, mobile and internet licence, thus increasing competition with the Chinese, who after the privatisation of the state telephone company SONITEL entered the Nigérien market, whose mobile penetration rate now stood at 5.5%.

Uranium represented an estimated 43% of export value. This was due to rising world prices as well as a new contract between Niger and Areva, signed on 13 January. Under the deal, Niger could sell 900 tonnes on its own account in both 2008 and 2009, while the contract price for uranium produced at the two existing mines at Arlit was increased by 50%. Areva was given approval for the development of the Imouraren mine, whose production was supposed to begin in 2010 and in due course to rise to an annual 5,000 tonnes of uranium oxide. This € 1 bn investment dwarfed the Chinese deal to develop another uranium mine (Teguidan Tessoumt). Imouraren could provide employment for around 1,400 permanent staff, and it was hoped that this and other mines would make Niger the world's number two uranium producer with an overall output of 9,000–10,000 tonnes a year. In reality, production fell by 8.2% in 2007 after it had increased 11% the year before, pushing Niger from fourth back to fifth place. The drop resulted from various factors, but Areva's obligation to maintain a higher level of security can only have increased costs. Despite the fall in production in 2007, the value of uranium exports rose as a result of the steep rise in world prices. The downward price trend during the second half of 2008 did not deter Areva from pressing ahead with its new site at Imouraren.

The China National Petroleum Corporation (CNPC) reached a deal in June for the development of *oil reserves* in the Agadem block, near the Chadian border. The CNPC's bid was first turned down as the company did not wish to commit itself to rapid exploration and the building of a refinery and pipeline linking to the Chad-Cameroon pipeline (the proven reserves of 300 million barrels were deemed insufficient for this). Yet the Chinese backtracked, indicating they suspected reserves to be larger.

The ECOWAS court of justice in April found the government guilty of failing to protect a child from *slavery*. Assisted by a British NGO, Hadjiatou Mani brought her case before the court, having been sold at the age of 12 and having been repeatedly raped and beaten by her master, whose children she bore. After ten years of slavery, which in Niger – as in other Sahelian countries – is akin to a kind of serfdom in a caste system, Mani was freed in 2005 following the criminalisation of slavery in 2003 (involving heavy fines and

prison terms of up to 30 years). The government, which was found
not guilty of legitimising slavery by enforcing customary law, vainly
argued that the case be thrown out as the woman had not exhausted
the national appeals process. It was ordered to pay compensation
of CFAfr 10 m (€ 15,000) and accepted the ruling. While the ruling
was a source of embarrassment, it did send out a signal about the
unacceptable nature of the entrenched practices that also existed in
other Sahelian countries, such as Mali (which as ECOWAS member
was now on notice) and notably Mauritania. In Niger, the local anti-
slavery society Timidria, claimed that 43,000 people were still living
as slaves, a figure that was disputed.

Niger in 2009

Concerns that President Tandja might extend his mandate by tampering with the constitution finally materialised. He dissolved the National Assembly and Constitutional Court, which had declared illegal a referendum on a three-year extension of his mandate. The plebiscite on the constitutional revision, boycotted by the opposition, was pushed through, as were parliamentary elections. Tandja's measures amounted to a constitutional coup d'état and split the political class, isolated Niger internationally and brought to an end a decade of stability under a multi-party dispensation. At year's end, rumours surfaced about tensions in the armed forces, amidst efforts to tighten surveillance and appease the officer class with gifts. The Tuareg rebellion went into a downturn as a truce was announced in May, but this could not be consolidated. Kidnappings of Western nationals pointed to rising insecurity in the Saharan zone.

New calculations of growth in 2008 reported a record rate of 9.5%, thanks to a boost in agricultural output – much higher than previously calculated. The growth rate for 2009 was expected to decline significantly, in part as a result of the global economic downturn. The UNDP again put Niger at the bottom of its Human Development Index. Aid flows came into doubt as a result of Tandja's refusal to step down, although economic links with France and China remained solid.

Domestic Politics

Tandja's supporters in the ruling 'Mouvement National pour la Société du Développement' (MNSD) continued campaigning for a *third term* under the slogan 'Tazarce' (Hausa for 'continuity'). A memorandum was published calling on parliament to extend Tandja's second term by another three years. His supporters had initially aimed at a change in the constitution to allow for a full third term. They argued that the president needed time to resolve the Tuareg rebellion and to complete infrastructural projects. The new strategy would allow a continuation of his second term, while MPs would be given a similar *extension*. Initially, other parties declined to respond to the challenge of Tandja's kingmakers. These included the MNSD's coalition partner, the 'Convention Démocratique et Sociale' (CDS) of National Assembly chairman Mahaman Ousmane, and the opposition 'Parti Nigérien pour la Démocratie et le Socialisme' (PNDS) of Mahamadou Issoufou. In this vacuum, civil society organisations decided to take the lead, following on the establishment towards the end of 2008 of a coalition of 26 civic groups, parties and union federations called the 'Front Uni pour la Sauvegarde des Acquis Démocratiques' (FUSAD). Led by human rights campaigner Marou Amadou, it pledged to continue with its action.

One of the first moves by Tandja's supporters was to oust Hama Amadou from the MNSD chairmanship (21 February). Amadou, Tandja's rival presidential contender, was dismissed as prime minister in 2007 and imprisoned in 2008 on charges of embezzlement. Prime Minister Seyni Oumarou succeeded as MNSD chair, supported by new general secretary Albadé Abouba, the interior minister. On 27 March, during a visit to Niamey by French President Sarkozy, Tandja spoke against a change in the constitution. Despite this, on 5 May, two days after Tandja's meeting in Agadez with Tuareg rebels (the first since the conflict) and one day after his launch of the construction of the Imouraren uranium mine in the presence of France's development minister and the director of Areva (France's nuclear power company), the president called for a *constitutional referendum*. Behind this decision lay the fact that the current constitution exempted the article limiting presidential terms from revision by parliamentary vote or referendum. On 2 June, Tandja appointed a drafting committee, which proposed a presidential form of government instead of the existing semi-presidential one: the president would be the sole holder of executive power, appointing the cabinet and prime minister, formerly appointed by the Assembly. Tandja himself would have a transitional three-year term without an election, after which he would be allowed to renew his candidature in presidential polls indefinitely.

On 9 May, the 'Alliance Nigérienne pour la Démocratie et le Progrès' withdrew its support for Tandja, followed later by Mahaman Ousmane's CDS. Eight ministers resigned in the process. Mahamadou Issoufou's PNDS had already reacted early May, with a *demonstration* in Niamey that drew between 20,000 and 30,000 people. On 25 May, Tandja received a serious blow when the Constitutional Court ruled that a referendum about a third term was illegal. The following day, a furious Tandja dissolved the Assembly. On 29 May, the president broadcast to the nation that he would not be bound by the opinions of the Court or the Assembly but, on 12 June, the Court, undaunted, annulled as illegal a decree of 5 June calling the referendum. This reminded Tandja that any constitutional revision required the approval of fourth-fifths of the Assembly. A few days later, some 40,000 people demonstrated in the capital against the presidential plans and, on 24 June, Tandja submitted a request to the Constitutional Court to reconsider its position. However, when the president assumed *emergency powers* on 26 June, the Court again rejected his request, pointing out the necessity of parliamentary approval for a referendum, and bringing the number of negative rulings to three. At the end of the month, Tandja dissolved the Court and one week later appointed a new one.

If the titanic clash between the republic's institutions showed that the rule of law could not be done away with at a whim, the outcome amounted to a *constitutional coup d'état*. Tandja's behaviour showed that democratic values had not penetrated the political culture, especially among politicians who traced their origins to careers in the military. From 23 June, the army began to patrol the streets of the capital and, on 7 July, the chairman of the electoral commission announced the referendum for 4 August. Opposition parties, united in an umbrella organisation called the 'Front pour la Défense de la Démocratie' (FDD), withdrew their representatives from the commission. Legislative elections, which by law should take place within 90 days of the Assembly's dissolution, were set for 20 August but were subsequently postponed till 20 October.

In early June, the country's seven union federations decided to combine forces in the 'Intersyndicale des Travailleurs Nigériens'. Tandja knew that he could rely on support in the rural areas, where his regime enjoyed popularity as a result of small-scale development projects. Nevertheless, at the beginning of June, protests rocked the city of Dosso, south-east of Niamey, as demonstrators sacked government offices and vehicles and tried to attack the provincial chief's palace. The PNDS called for a referendum *boycott*, but the opposition failed to mobilise enough people for a 'pays mort' campaign on 1 July. On 13 July, Niger's lawyers staged a one-day strike to protest against the dissolution of the Constitutional Court and two days later about 100 women protesters were dispersed with batons and tear gas during a sit-in at the Court. Tandja's supporters began to organise increasing numbers of counter-demonstrations. Mahamadou Issoufou of the PNDS was briefly detained by the gendarmerie on 30 June when he called on the army to disobey Tandja's orders, while FUSAD leader Marou Amadou was arrested about the same time on charges of sedition. A number of high-ranking officers assured Tandja that the military would remain neutral. On 3 July, the president issued a decree by which judges opposed to his plans were transferred to remote posts in the countryside.

The state media began a 'Yes' campaign, to which trade unions responded by calling a *general strike* on 23–24 July. On 4 August – referendum day – numerous demonstrators were arrested in the city of Tahoua, in the centre of the country. On 30 July, prosecutors issued an international arrest warrant for Hama Amadou, who had gone abroad (he had been provisionally released to undergo medical treatment in France). Marou Amadou of FUSAD was rearrested on 10 August for having called for the overthrow of the Tandja regime. The *referendum* itself was a non-event, as so often in the modern history of the country. According to the electoral commission, turnout was 68%, of which 92.5% approved the new constitution. The 'Coordination des Forces pour la Démocratie et la République' (CFDR), a body now combining unions, civic groups, the CDS, ANDP and PNDS into an extra-parliamentary opposition force, claimed the turnout barely reached 5% and that the outcome was null and void. The new Constitutional Court confirmed the results.

Ahead of the parliamentary elections on 20 October, the government began investigations targeting dozens of MPs on suspicion of *corruption*. An inspection of the accounts of the Assembly (known to be a rich source of perks) showed that millions of euros had gone missing, but the investigations were obviously an attempt to silence Tandja's opponents. Over the course of several weeks, more than 120 politicians were charged with misappropriation of funds, including Mahamadou Issoufou of the PNDS and Assembly chair Mahamane Ousmane. At the time, the latter was presiding at a session of the ECOWAS parliament in Abuja and was therefore driven into exile – like Hama Amadou. All three were *political tycoons* with long-standing careers and a dislike of each other, but they were now driven into each other's arms. Issoufou left Niger for ECOWAS-sponsored talks. When he returned home on 30 October, he faced an arrest warrant, but was not arrested. It was not only opposition politicians who fell victim to harassment, but also members of the independent media. Abdoulaye Tiémogo of the private 'Le Canard Déchaîné' was given a three-month jail sentence on 18 August for "casting discredit on a judicial ruling" and, during the same month, the directors of eight weeklies were questioned over articles accusing the president's son of taking bribes.

The CFDR forum called for a boycott of the *legislative elections* and for a protest gathering on 26 September in Niamey. On 21 September, Prime Minister Seyni Oumarou and two of his colleagues – staunch Tandja supporters – resigned in order to stand in the parliamentary elections. The president appointed Ali Badio Gamatié, a former finance minister and World Bank technocrat, to replace Seyni Oumarou. The MNSD took 76 of the 113 seats and five smaller parties allied to the MNSD took another 25. Eleven independents also gained seats, a disappointment for Tandja's opponents since they represented the only opposition in the Assembly. The Constitutional Court validated the results. The alleged turnout was 51.3%; some reports suggest that turnout in the countryside was high, but this was disputed by the opposition and some international observers, who reported an overall low turnout. The military, who voted one day ahead of the polls, abstained in massive numbers – as had happened during the referendum.

A CFDR-sponsored meeting in Niamey on 13 December drew thousands of demonstrators. Two days later, Tandja retaliated with a counter-demonstration, and a union-sponsored gathering at the university later that month underlined the high level of political *tensions*. On 24 December, the government delegation to ECOWAS-mediated talks with the opposition walked out after the West African body stated that 22 December marked the end of Tandja's legal tenure. The opposition had agreed to talks as a concession when the government suspended the arrest warrants on Hama Amadou and Mahamadou Issoufou. The warrants were reactivated and Mahaman Ousmane also became subject to arrest. New talks were scheduled for 7 January. On 27 December, Tandja completed his constitutional coup with *local elections*, which were boycotted by the opposition and disapproved of by the international community. Representatives for 265 councils were elected and the MNSD predictably captured over half the seats, the remainder taken by parties participating in the ruling coalition.

Security in the north remained a problem. On 22 January, four Western citizens returning from a festival on nomad culture were kidnapped in the border zone with Mali. Rumours continued about the *kidnapping* the previous December of the UN special envoy to Niger, Robert Fowler, his aide, Louis Guay – both Canadian, and their local driver, in the vicinity of the capital. A video showing the three captives was released in Bamako on 30 January. Niger's government pointed the finger at Tuareg rebels, but the main 'Mouvement des Nigériens pour la Justice' (MJN) denied responsibility. Another rebel faction, the 'Front des Forces de Redressement' (FFR), had first claimed responsibility but later retracted. Fowler's driver was released in Mali in late March. His kidnappers, sub-contractors, had handed the three over to members of 'Al-Qaida in the Land of the Islamic Maghreb', the Algeria-based group of Islamist activists, which on 28 March demanded the release of 20 of its members by Mali and other countries in exchange for Fowler and the other five Westerners. Fowler and his fellow Canadian, together with two of the Western tourists captured in January (a German and a Swiss woman) were released on 22 April. A ransom may have been paid, although the Canadian government denied this. Later in September, Fowler suggested that the Niger government might have been in-volved in his kidnapping, since it deeply resented his mediation mission in the Tuareg rebellion and his capture had occurred in a safe zone. If true, this would exacerbate the already grim picture of Tandja's regime. In the course of the year, one of the hostages taken in January, a Briton, was murdered by his captors; they had demanded the release of a Jordanian from a UK prison, which the British refused. The remaining Westerner was released later, but an-other incident rocked Niger on 28 December: roughly in the same area where the other incidents took place, three Saudi tourists were killed by gunmen, while several others were injured. Three suspects were arrested.

The splintering in the ranks of the *Tuareg rebels* continued. In March, Aklu Sidisidi led a group of rebels to leave the MJN and form a third faction, the 'Front Patriotique Nigérien' (FPN). In April, possi-bly encouraged by the weakening of the rebel ranks, the government sent a security official to Libya to negotiate a truce – a clear softening of its line. The previous week, a group of rebels had announced that it planned to surrender its weapons after a call for a truce by Libya's leader Col. Kadhafi. These manoeuvres led to direct talks between Niger's government and Tuareg rebels – the first since the eruption

of the conflict – in Tripoli on 5–6 April. Interior Minister Abouba
met representatives of all three factions. While all sides agreed to
make peace, the accord, which involved rebel disarmament, a general amnesty, the lifting of the state of alert and release of detainees,
was stalled. The MJN questioned Niamey's commitment to peace
and reiterated demands, such as a greater share by the Tuareg population in the country's uranium proceeds. On 3 May, Tandja himself
met in Agadez with representatives of the three rebel factions, who,
before the meeting, announced the release of the last government
soldier still held hostage. Tandja promised the rebels an amnesty in
exchange for laying down their arms, but no date was set for the
signing of an accord or the disarmament process. On 15 May, after
talks with the prime minister, the MJN and FPN agreed to a ceasefire,
but the FFR boycotted these talks.

Disagreement within the rebel ranks thus beset the elaboration
of an agreement. On 31 August, the MJN, which called on the other
factions to regroup, announced that it had deposed its own leader, Aghaly Ag Alamba, accusing him of spending too much time in
Libyan hotels. The other factions reiterated demands, such as the release of prisoners, posts in the armed forces and a share in uranium
proceeds. On 5–6 October, several rebels, deprived of Libyan support, felt forced to agree to a formal ending of the conflict at Sabha
in Libya. The MJN said that Libya had exceeded its powers as mediator, and both MJN and FFR, disappointed by the government's refusal to concede a bigger share in uranium proceeds and more jobs
for Tuaregs in the army and the mining sector, swore to continue the
struggle. With only the FPN and the MJN's deposed Aghaly Alambo
as signatories, the accord's future remained dubious. Nevertheless,
the government announced an amnesty and the lifting of the state
of alert. Around 800 rebels in Libya were planning to return home.
So far, the conflict had cost the lives of some 400 people, wounded
many more and displaced some 20,000 civilians.

Towards the end of the year, reports trickled in about tension in
the *armed forces*. On 10 November, with soldiers dissatisfied about

the sharp reduction in pay brought about by a decrease in mission indemnities earned during the Tuareg rebellion, the chief of staff warned them not to engage in politics. Pamphlets circulated asserting that the president's tenure after 22 December was illegitimate. Although Tandja had increased gifts to the military, rumours of coup plots surfaced and a dozen young officers were questioned. The assistant chief of staff of the army, who had resisted presidential bribes, had already been replaced. With a presidential guard increased to 600 men, commanded by a fellow easterner, the president's security was stepped up considerably.

Foreign Affairs

Foreign policy was dominated by the fall-out from Tandja's takeover. On 15 May, a delegation of the Council of the Wise of ECOWAS pointed out to the president that he had signed a protocol banning electoral reform without majority support within six months of an election. The following day, ECOWAS issued a sanctions threat and, on 24 August, its Mediation and Security Council in Abuja expressed concern over the violation of Niger's constitution, establishing an ad hoc committee of four countries (Nigeria, Benin, Burkina Faso and Sierra Leone) to confer with Nigérien stakeholders. A special summit in Abuja on 17 October called for postponement of the parliamentary elections, also banning Niger from putting up candidates for posts in international organisations and hosting ECOWAS meetings. A delegation led by Liberia's President Sirleaf could not dissuade Tandja from his collision course and, when the elections went ahead, Niger's membership was suspended. However, mediation continued. On 10 November, the ECOWAS mediator, Nigerian Ret. General Abubakar, met a 22-member delegation of Niger's government in Abuja, followed by a similar meeting two days later with opposition representatives, and, on 13 December, Abubakar travelled to Niamey for a dialogue with all parties concerned. With the passing of the 22 December constitutional deadline, ECOWAS issued its statement on the end of Tandja's legal mandate, to which the government responded with a walkout.

In November, the EU froze non-humanitarian development aid to the value of € 458 m. The US also reacted sharply, but not being Niger's principal trading partner and focusing strongly on anti-terrorist issues in the Sahara, Washington's influence was circumscribed. When the 22 December limit of Tandja's tenure passed, it refused to recognise the president's legitimacy. The next day it suspended non-humanitarian aid and imposed travel restrictions on members of the regime. If the result of these measures was limited, their symbolism in terms of Niger's international isolation was powerful. *Nigeria*, one of Niger's principal trading partners, also expressed concern, temporarily closing the border in November. Since transport through Nigeria is of crucial importance to Niger's landlocked economy, this could be interpreted as a warning signal.

Tandja, however, could rely on support from Libya, France and China. *Libya*'s leader, Kadhafi, having been asked to help end the rebellion, put pressure on rebel factions. On 12 March, he made a stopover in Niamey, handing over army soldiers held hostage by rebels. He facilitated the talks between the government and rebel factions in Tripoli in April. However, he clearly went too far in pressing the rebels, and some later repudiated the peace deal. Tandja visited Libya in person early in September. *France* trod a delicate line between disapproval of Tandja's moves and not wishing to endanger imports of Niger's uranium – representing 38% of French uranium imports (expected to rise to 50% by 2012). During his visit to Niger on 27 March, Sarkozy said that he did not favour life presidencies but also made it clear that he would not interfere. The fact that Tandja made his referendum call the day after the launching of the construction of the Imouraren uranium mine in the presence of the French development minister and Areva's director showed that French support was crucial. Some sources suggested Tandja secured discrete backing from Sarkozy, though this may not have been more than reluctant acquiescence. The *Chinese* felt no compunction in maintaining ties with Niamey, the vice president of the China National Petroleum Corporation visiting Niger on 30 July and being received with full honours. Chinese comments on political events remained moderate.

Other issues in foreign relations included the rising insecurity in the Saharan zone. On 6 September, the press reported a meeting of army representatives of Niger, Mali and Mauritania with their counterparts in *Algeria* to discuss plans to counter terrorism and cross-border crime.

Socioeconomic Developments

New calculations of GDP *growth* in 2008 yielded a much higher figure: 9.5%, mainly caused by a growth of 25% to 30% in cereal produce. However, forecasts for 2009 warned of a sharp drop in growth. It was estimated that inflation would fall from a year-on-year rate of more than 10% to around 5% due to lower import prices and the excellent 2008 harvest (4.96 m tonnes of cereals), but this year's *harvest* was far poorer than in 2008. Confronted with erratic rainfall (there was flooding in some regions, destroying some 3,500 homes), many areas saw disappointing crop yields, presaging malnutrition or starvation in the coming year.

The *uranium* sector saw the start of the construction of the Imouraren mine, with 67% owned by Areva and the remainder in the hands of the Nigérien state. Uranium exports for 2009–2010 were predicted to increase in value as a result of the higher contract price negotiated with Areva in 2008. Market prices also increased – 35% up by June – as a result of the new global popularity of nuclear energy. This could boost Niger's overall growth.

On 3 July, Niger, Nigeria and Algeria signed an agreement in Abuja on the building of a gas pipeline across the Sahara for the export of Nigerian gas to North Africa. Work started on the Kandadji dam,

intended to produce power and water for irrigation. The Chinese
were awarded the first major contract in this huge project; they also
began work on the construction of the oil refinery in Zinder, to be
fed by the Agadem block near the Chadian border, and were already
working on the second bridge across the Niger river in Niamey. In
2008, *Chinese trade* with Niger increased fivefold.

In the course of the year, Niger was granted *development aid* by
various donors but it was unclear whether these plans would be affected by the political developments. Some of the programmes that
were hit included the money to be provided by the EU, with which
Niger signed six agreements in May worth some $ 300 m in terms of
budget support.

The government renationalised the national telecommunications company, SONITEL, after a Chinese-Libyan consortium own-
ing a stake of 51% had failed to abide by the contract, notably with
regard to modernisation of the network. Despite its mining attractions, the 'Doing Business Report' of the World Bank ranked Niger
at 174 out of 183 countries in terms of its *business environment.* Its
poor rating was affected by the degree of red tape and strict labour
regulations. Some hope was placed in the peace deal with Tuareg
rebels and the boost this could give to tourism, which depends on
the attractions of the northern region.

The UNDP again put Niger at the bottom of its Human
Development Index. With life expectancy at 50 and school enrolment stalled at 27.2% and adult literacy at 28.7% – low even for West
Africa, Niger was statistically a worse place to live than Afghanistan.
The government claimed the report was based on erroneous population estimates. In March, around 30 people died after an outbreak
of meningitis, which began in neighbouring Nigeria. Casualties
climbed to over 200. The EU donated € 4.7 m to assist in coping with
the epidemic.

Niger in 2010

Political, social and economic developments contributed to an eventful year. In February a coup d'état ended President Tandja's hold on power, itself the result of a constitutional putsch in 2009 that aimed to perpetuate his rule by illegal means. The military's action seemed to confirm its unofficial role as guardian of the constitutional order – as in 1999, when a putsch heralded the return to civilian rule. The junta detained the president while beginning discussions with representatives of civil society on the modalities of a transition period that should return the country to constitutional rule within the year. Sections of the political class became the object of an anticorruption drive and a new constitution was drawn up in a process of broad-based consultations and successfully put to the vote in October. Before the year was out, local elections had taken place ahead of legislative and presidential polls scheduled for early 2011. The economy was affected by a sharp fall in external budget aid and famine conditions resulting from the disappointing harvest of 2009. The situation turned into a humanitarian crisis worse than in 2005. Aid came late, while the new rainy season resulted in floods, leaving thousands of people homeless, destroying crops and drowning livestock, which had already suffered badly from the 2009 drought. The government broke with Tandja's policy of denial of Niger's vulnerability to famine, while the rains presaged a better harvest for 2010. The security situation in the Saharan zone deteriorated, with Tuareg kidnappers, working on behalf of al-Qaida in the (Land of the) Islamic Maghreb (AQIM), becoming more brazen in targeting Western nationals. The previous year's truce with Tuareg rebel factions held, although it was not tied up in a formal agreement. The junta substantially improved the country's foreign relations, ending international isolation and achieving the progressive resumption of aid. It celebrated the 50th anniversary of Independence in appropriately modest fashion.

Domestic Politics

Early in the year Nigeria's General (retired) Abubakar, appointed by
ECOWAS to mediate an end to the crisis between Tandja and the
opposition, proposed a 'road map' envisaging a transition unity
government. However, talks between Tandja's side and the opposition were suspended on 11 February without reaching agreement.
On 18 February, the army ended the year-long crisis by removing
Tandja's regime in a well organised *coup d'état*. As the president was
chairing a cabinet meeting that had brought almost all government
ministers to the palace, troops and tanks overseen by helicopters
attacked the presidential guards. Weakened by an infiltration of
their ranks, the guards had to surrender, although not without several hours of fighting that left between three and a dozen people
dead. A perplexed Tandja was brought to a military barracks before
being moved to a building inside the presidential grounds. The illegal extension of his reign had been cut short less than two months
after it had begun, on 22 December the previous year. Tandja's constitution, doctored in 2009, was suspended and government institutions were replaced by what was called the 'Conseil Suprême pour
la Restauration de la Démocratie' (CSRD) led by Major Salou Djibo,
a squadron leader responsible for the tank regiment. He was backed
by three colonels who had already taken part in the coup restoring
civilian rule in 1999.

Whilst some corporate issues played a background role in pushing the military into action, the primary reason for the army's move
was the desire to put an end to the country's political crisis and
international isolation. Three days after the coup, the junta issued
a statement promising the drafting of a new constitution and the
holding of elections. It did not immediately set out a schedule, but
in the course of the year it became clear that it would do its best to
have the process completed within 12 months of its putsch. Djibo,
a taciturn military man, let it be known that his programme con-
sisted of a clean-up of the political system (by now rotten to the

core through the corruption of Tandja's hangers-on), national reconciliation and the military's return to barracks after elections. On
20 February, jubilant crowds greeted the military's move with *demonstrations of support* in the capital Niamey, as well as in Dosso and
Tahoua.

On 1 March, Djibo appointed a civilian prime minister,
Mahamadou Danda, a neutral technocrat who had served in an administration a decade earlier but had pursued a diplomatic career
since then. The junta leader provided Danda with a *new cabinet*
that lacked politicians but included unknown technocrats and administrators, as well as people who had stayed abroad for extended
periods, and a few army officers. On 12 March, the CSRD issued a
decree banning cabinet and junta members from standing in the
prospective elections, a prohibition that extended to other members of the military, the police and gendarmerie, customs officers,
and employees of some parastatals. Another decree issued a similar
ban for regional governors (now newly appointed military officers),
district administrators and the country's chiefs – these last tainted
by their association with Tandja.

On 2 April, a 131-strong 'Conseil Consultatif National' (CCN)
was formed to advise on and guide the *transition process*, while a
'Comité des textes fondamentaux' was to draft a new constitution,
an electoral code and regulations governing the status of political
parties. Headed by Marou Amadou, the human rights campaigner
who had played a prominent role in the opposition to Tandja, the
CCN included diverse civil society groups as well as members of the
military and political parties. After a week of talks, it proposed a
transition schedule that was to end with presidential elections on 26
December and 26 January 2011, with civilian rule being restored by
1 March 2011, slightly longer than the proposed 12 months after the
coup. On 5 May, the junta accepted these proposals, which included
a referendum on the constitution. The 'Comité des textes fondamentaux' was charged with presenting a new constitution within
45 days, aimed at assuring the country's political and institutional

stability. In addition, the junta established a 'Conseil constitution-nel' to replace the Constitutional Court that had consistently stood in the way of Tandja's moves the previous year and, as a conse-quence, had been dissolved in its original composition. In addition, Salou Djibo appointed an 'Observatoire national de la communica-tion' to improve the status of the media, which had suffered consid-erably under the previous government's harassment.

The proposals for a *new constitution* caused controversy among members of the political class, as they included such novelties as age limits for presidential candidates (a minimum of 35 and maxi-mum of 70 years), the stipulation that they should have a second-ary school certificate plus some higher education (which would disqualify Tandja's former prime minister, Seyni Oumarou) and the requirement of a CFAfr 10 m deposit. MPs, too, would face age limits and educational requirements. Presidential terms and parliamen-tary mandates would be reduced to four years (the presidential term renewable only once). In the end, the educational requirements were dropped, as was the maximum age limit, and the presidential term remained at five years renewable once only. The new consti-tution reduced the powers of the head of state while increasing those of the prime minister and boosting the independence of the judiciary. It also reaffirmed commitment to international rules on democracy and human rights – an area where the country's repu-tation had been severely damaged by Tandja's demeanour – while providing the junta leaders with immunity from prosecution over their coup d'état.

Tandja's cabinet ministers were released from custody or house arrest within two days of the putsch, with the exception of Prime Minister Ali Badio Gamatié, Interior Minister Albadé Abouba, and Finance Minister Lamine Zeine, all Tandja confidants. Gamatié and Zeine were set free a little later. On 28 March, the junta (re-)arrested around 20 people including some military, who had refused to join the putschists, and Seyni Oumarou and Lamine Zeine, after they had pressed for Tandja's release. A couple of days later, most were set free again and put under temporary house arrest. The junta's reference to state security as the reason for keeping Tandja and his interior minister behind bars could not be simply dismissed, as it was reported that Tandja remained unrepentant, as did many of his stalwarts in the 'Mouvement National pour la Société du Développement' (MNSD). Tandja asked permission to leave for Tunisia for medical treatment, which was turned down. However, the ECOWAS court of justice, which received a complaint from Tandja's family, judged on 8 November that *Tandja's continued detention* was illegal, and ordered his release. Government lawyers said they would appeal. While it was ironical that an institution of ECOWAS – an organisation that Tandja had cold-shouldered the previous year – came to the former president's defence, the result was that the new government decided to have him formally prosecuted on corruption charges, for which a court lifted his immunity towards year's end.

On 14 June, the government introduced a new independent electoral commission of 50 members tasked with organising the plebiscite and elections. This also included the drafting of a timetable and the revision of the electoral register, which was said to be biased in favour of Tandja and needed the inclusion of youths who had turned 18 in the previous two years, among others. This process led to the inclusion of 600,000 new names on a register of six million and was completed on 1 October. With a French grant of CFAfr 600 m, the commission set up the modalities for the *referendum* of 31 October, which led to a 'yes' vote of more than 90% with a turnout of 52.65% – high by Nigérien standards. The results were confirmed by the constitutional council and, on 25 November, Djibo approved the new constitution, which would lead to Niger's seventh republic. While a textbook transition so far, which in itself constituted a sharp break with the authoritarianism of the previous regime, the remainder of the electoral schedule had to be revised in view of organisational problems, setting new dates for local, parliamentary and presidential elections in January 2011, with the support of civil society and the political parties. At year's end, the presidential candidatures of all major politicians had been approved, including of Tandja's ex-prime minister, Seyni Oumarou.

The junta also began an *anti-corruption purge* among politicians and Tandja appointees in state and parastatal institutions. A 'commission de lutte contre la délinquance économique, financière et fiscale et pour la promotion de la bonne gouvernance', with powers to confiscate assets, was established on 12 May. Although donors pointed out the risk of arbitrariness and doubts remained about its effectiveness over the long term, TI welcomed these steps. The junta announced it would investigate the state's past financial affairs, notably the granting of mining exploration permits and privatisations. On 20 April, it sacked 20 officials of state-owned companies responsible for oil and uranium exploration, among others. All were personal appointees of Tandja and, while the MNSD cried foul, the opaque manner in which many of the president's cronies had been put into lucrative positions required action if the change of regime was to have some effect. Judicial police detained a former mines minister in June, as well as Hadia Toulaye Tandja (the president's son), a journalist and an official of the mining ministry for corruption and money laundering in relation to uranium exploration licences (about which rumours had circulated the previous year). On 2 August, former Prime Minister Seyni Oumarou was detained for four days on embezzlement charges and then released on bail. Others, too, met this fate, including Finance Minister Lamine Zeine and top civil servants and directors of parastatals. It was admitted that the junta's methods were brutal, but it was pointed out that CFAfr 2 bn had already been recuperated by 31 July. Seyni Oumarou was reported to have paid back a substantial sum of money. As was to be expected, most of the people involved were from in and around the MNSD. The measures met with broad approval.

Most other members of the *political class* kept quiet, intent on jockeying for position ahead of the 2011 elections. The key parties were still united in the 'Coordination des Forces pour la Démocratie et la République' (CFDR), a common front established the previous year to oppose Tandja's coup. In the course of the year, party leaders who had gone into exile in 2009 all returned home: Hama Amadou, one-time secretary-general of the MNSD who had fallen out with Tandja (and now established his own political vehicle); Mahamane Ousmane of the 'Convention Démocratique et Sociale'; and Mahamadou Issoufou of the left-wing 'Parti Nigérien pour la Démocratie et le Socialisme'. The MNSD held its party congress on 7–8 August, at the end of which it elected Seyni Oumarou as its candidate for the presidential polls of 2011, while the other parties united in the CFDR resolved to put forward a single candidate.

Optimism about the political future remained intact, although for a short while it seemed threatened by a couple of military-related incidents. On 16 October, and in the following days Col. Abdoulaye Badié, Djibo's permanent secretary and a powerful figure responsible for the army's finances, was arrested together with three other officers including Djibo's intelligence chief and the equipment minister. On 22 October, the government said the officers had opposed the return to democracy and decided to challenge the junta's decisions. It is true that *coup rumours* had been circulating and security been tightened, but nothing more emerged over this than that there had been differences over the electoral timetable. While personal relations between Djibo and Badié had deteriorated, it seems doubtful that any tangible plans for a coup had been made.

With the February coup, the *human rights* situation had the potential to improve, although in the end resistance in civil society and the political class prevented the abolition of the death penalty (the last executions took place in the 1970s). The media climate improved markedly, however. Having suffered under the intolerant Tandja, media leaders were invited to a conference to help devise a new framework for the press, leading to the decriminalisation of defamation. Sahara FM, a radio station in the uranium town of Arlit, restarted broadcasting on 14 June after having been shut down over its coverage of the Tuareg rebellion.

Early in January, with Tandja still at the helm of the state, the main faction of the *Tuareg rebels*, the 'Mouvement des Nigériens pour la Justice', formally handed over weapons and vehicles at a ceremony in Arlit, with one of its leaders, Aghaly Alambo, expressing willingness to co-operate with the government. Rebel leaders gained the right to participate in the deliberations of the CCN guiding the transition process, while a new authority for national reconciliation was set up on 15 April to help in the normalisation of life (thousands of rebels still awaited demobilisation). However, one faction leader, Rhissa Ag Boula of the 'Front des Forces de Redressement', was arrested at the end of March by the new junta, together with one of his rebel allies. Boula had been sentenced to death over his alleged involvement with the murder of an MNSD militant in 2004 and, as a consequence, was not covered by the general amnesty from which all the other leaders now benefited.

Security in the Saharan zone deteriorated further. In the third week of April, a French and an Algerian national were kidnapped at I-n-Abangharit, south-west of Arlit, with the Algerian driver later being released and the Frenchman, a 78-year-old retired engineer involved in development work, brought to an AQIM stronghold in northern Mali. He was murdered in July after a French-Mauritanian operation to free him was botched. On 16 September, a spectacular *kidnapping* took place in Arlit, when around 30 armed men arrived with several pick-up trucks at the homes of seven civilians (four Frenchmen, one Frenchwoman, a Togolese and a Malagasy working for French nuclear giant Areva and an engineering group) and made off with their hostages to the Timétrine, an inhospitable region in Mali marked by table mountains and caves, which was a refuge for smugglers and bandit operations. Security was stepped up amidst recriminations between Niger and France over the lapse in security. The French sent 80 military personnel, surveillance plane(s) and a jet fighter to help in the search for the hostages, now claimed to be in the hands of AQIM, while the junta saw to a massive reinforcement of security in Arlit.

Foreign Affairs

The *international response to the coup d'état* was muted. As relations
with Niger had been seriously damaged by Tandja's constitutional
putsch the previous year, it was realised that things could not get
much worse. The AU nevertheless condemned the coup and un-
helpfully suspended Niger's membership, demanding elections
within six months. ECOWAS, too, demanded a swift return to constitutional rule and a troika mission of ECOWAS, AU and the UN immediately flew to Niamey for reassurances. Niger's membership of
ECOWAS was restored in July (albeit as an observer). The UN also
condemned the coup, but pointedly noted that Tandja was as much
to blame. In September, Salou Djibo was allowed to participate in
the UN Millennium Summit in New York. Relations with France
were expected to improve, as under Tandja these had suffered over
a host of issues, and Salou Djibo was quickly invited to take part in
the Franco-African summit (31 May–1 June), while his wife figured
prominently in the company of Carla Bruni, President Sarkozy's
wife, at a photo session with African first ladies celebrating 50 years
of African independence on Bastille Day.

Ties with the EU had priority as the aid cut over Tandja's putsch
began to cripple the economy (donor aid making up half the government budget). While the EU provided funds for the organisation
of the elections to a value of € 16.3 m, Prime Minister Mahamadou
Danda's mission to Brussels in May led to a decision to progressively
resume budgetary support as well as to restart the disbursement in
steps of € 368 m under the tenth EDF, which had been frozen the
previous year.

The coup d'état put relations with *China* in some doubt, as the
Chinese had not joined the criticism of Tandja (one of his sons being
commercial attaché in Hong Kong). With media reports coming in
about poor conditions for Nigériens working for Chinese companies, and suggestions that their opaque contracts with the state concerning oil and uranium exploration needed scrutiny, in addition

to the fact that under Tandja they had enjoyed direct access to the presidential office, the Chinese position in Niger did not improve. However, with China's trade with Niger growing by more than 50% as compared to 2009 alone, it remained doubtful whether the junta could adopt a more critical view of the economic role played by the Chinese.

Relations with neighbouring countries were dominated by the *regional security threat* posed by AQIM and its subcontractors. In April, it was reported that Niger, Mali, Mauritania and Algeria would set up a joint command centre in Tamanrasset to co-ordinate intelligence gathering. Military chiefs from the four countries met in the southern Algerian town on 26 September, officials of the same countries having met on 15 September in Algiers to agree on improved coordination of border surveillance. In mid-October, Niger participated in a meeting with Sahelian and G8 countries in Bamako to discuss the AQIM threat.

Socioeconomic Developments

Growth was forecast to climb back to over 3%, having dropped sharply the previous year into negative figures as a result of the disappointing cereal harvest. As a result of the EU sanctions, the government had to slash the 2010 budget by 13%, though it said on 4 May that this would not affect salaries.

The 30% drop in cereal production in 2009 was expected to cause both humanitarian and macroeconomic problems (40% of GDP being dependent on the agricultural sector). With *cereal shortages* of 410,000 tonnes and much livestock having died, WFP planned to feed some 850,000 people during the lean season (March–October), but then increased the target to 1.7 m. However, it was estimated earlier that more than half the population – some 7.8 m people – would go without food if they did not receive aid. Fortunately, the junta immediately reversed Tandja's policy of denial, opening the field for collaboration with humanitarian agencies, and appealed for some $ 123 m in food aid. In the spring it was estimated that some 2.7 m people were highly food insecure and another 5.1 m moderately food insecure but, regrettably, international pledges were slow in coming. By June only 46% of the food appeal had been covered.

The growing *famine* caused people to flock to the cities, with a sharp rise reported in prostitution and crime. Many trekked to neighbouring countries such as Nigeria, but little succour in terms of food or jobs could be found there. Called the epicentre of the crisis in the Sahelian zone, Niger reported an overall acute malnutrition rate of over 16% for those under the age of five (i.e. above the 15% warning threshold). The EU provided another € 24 m for food aid to the Sahel in early June, while USAID announced help worth $ 66 m. Special programmes were launched to feed nomadic communities. On 20 July, WFP said it would boost its aid, expecting to feed some 7.9 m people by the end of the year. In August, it was claimed that one in five children in the age group 0–3 were now acutely undernourished. The Red Cross estimated that 70% of livestock in the Sahelian region were threatened. Endebtedness increased among peasants, who were forced to sell off future harvests to traders, causing fears about depleted grain reserves in the year to come. The junta began the distribution of food free of charge to around a million people, creating a special food security agency to oversee the practicalities. After the Tandja years, these measures were unprecedented.

In the autumn, famine conditions began to diminish, thanks to the abundant rains. No reliable figures were available about deaths caused by famine or malnutrition. The rains led to serious *flooding*. Crops were destroyed and livestock drowned (the UN giving a figure of 30,000 animals), while tens of thousands of people were said to have lost their homes. The Tillabéri region was one of the worst affected areas. On the whole, however, the cereal harvest was much better than in the previous year.

WFP reported that 59.9% of the population were living below the poverty datum line and, although life expectancy had now grown by 24% since 1989 as a result of government efforts to improve health care and food security, the drop in GDP per capita over the previous two decades meant that the overall *quality of life* remained dismally low.

The government agreed to study with Benin projected plans for the extension of the Cotonou-Parakou *railway* (jointly owned by them) to link up with the city of Dosso. Traffic between the two countries had grown considerably in the preceding years, benefiting from Niger's free access to the port of Cotonou, among other things.

The Chinese-run *uranium* mine at Teguidan Tessoumt was expected to go into operation. In November, Areva announced that it would form a partnership with South Korea's state electricity company to operate the large Imouraren mine, whose opening was pushed back to 2013–14. Uranium prices increased as global demands again began to outstrip supply. In 2009, Niger's production, accounting for half of its exports, increased by 7%. Towards year's end, Areva had to admit to the veracity of accusations by Greenpeace that radiation levels in Arlit's sister city of Akokan were unacceptably high. Earlier it had declared the city's streets safe, yet at one location radiation was 500 times higher than the normal background level.

China began work on the 600 km pipeline to transport *oil* from the Agadem block near the Chadian border to a refinery being constructed in Zinder. Not unexpectedly, on 2 August the junta announced approval of the accords with the Chinese.

Niger in 2011

Presidential and legislative elections concluded a successful return to civilian rule. The new president, long-time opposition leader Mahamadou Issoufou, gained a precarious hold on power as it would be difficult to keep all the promises made on the economic front and sections of the military remained unruly. In the summer, there was another coup threat, followed by several arrests. At the start of the year, a kidnapping incident involving two young Frenchmen rocked the capital and underlined the deterioration of security in the Sahelian region, made worse by the violent overthrow of the Kadhafi regime in Libya. A catastrophic harvest further complicated the country's food security and presaged famine for 2012. General economic prospects for 2012 were boosted by the beginning of oil production and the start-up of a new uranium mine.

Domestic Politics

Ahead of the parliamentary and presidential elections scheduled to finalise the transition to civilian rule, the party alliance, 'Coordination des Forces pour la Démocratie et la République' (CFDR), came apart. The CFDR had been formed in 2009 to oppose the continued hold on power by President Tandja – deposed in 2010 by the military for his constitutional putsch the previous year – and that of his party, the 'Mouvement National pour la Société du Développement' (MNSD). *Local elections*, delayed into 2011 as a result of logistical problems, preceded the general contest on 11 January. While 80% of council seats were taken by the country's four principal parties, the results signalled an end to the dominance of the MNSD, essentially in place since the end of the Cold War. The opposition 'Parti Nigérien pour la Démocratie et le Socialisme' (PNDS) of Mahamadou Issoufou gained the largest number of council seats. The MNSD lost half its

© KONINKLIJKE BRILL NV, LEIDEN, 2019 | DOI:10.1163/9789004401440_005

usual vote and came second and, surprisingly, the new 'Mouvement Démocratique Nigérien' (Moden-Lumana) of one-time MNSD colleague and rival of Mamadou Tandja, Hama Amadou, came third, cutting deep into the western region, from where the new MNSD leader – Tandja confidant Seyni Oumarou – hailed. The 'Convention Démocratique et Sociale' (CDS) of former National Assembly chair Mahamane Ousmane trailed behind.

The relative decline of the MNSD sealed the fate of the CFDR pact. On 25 January, before the legislative elections and the first round of the presidentials – to be held on 31 January – Hama Amadou and Mahamane Ousmane broke with the PNDS and formed a new alliance with the MNSD called 'Alliance pour la Réconciliation Nationale' (ARN). They and Seyni Oumarou promised to support whichever of them would make it to the presidential run-off. Isolating Mahamadou Issoufou, this *reversal of alliance* was meant to limit the damage to Ousmane's CDS and maintain Hama Amadou's influence, but it was condemned in the media – the MNSD had, after all, become tainted by Tandja's 2009 constitutional coup.

The local elections had already shown that, despite its decline, the MNSD could not be completely written off, and the general elections on 31 January confirmed this. In addition to Mahamane Issoufou, Seyni Oumarou, Hama Amadou and Mahamane Ousmane (all but Oumarou long-time established figures), six more people joined the race, including civil society activist Bayard Mariama Gamatié, Niger's first female presidential contender. PNDS leader Mahamadou Issoufou gained the upper hand with 36.1% of the vote, followed by Seyni Oumarou with 23.2% and Hama Amadou with 19.8%. Mahamane Ousmane, whose activism had declined in the course of Tandja's putsch, gained 8.3%, and the other candidates still less. In the *parliamentary polls*, the PNDS won a clear 34 seats (out of 113), doubling the number of its MPs in the National Assembly, followed by the MNSD and the new Moden of Hama Amadou. The CDS was practically annihilated. The remainder of the seats were shared between a couple of lesser parties.

With turnout hovering around the 50% mark, the parliamentary landscape had been thoroughly redrawn, making Hama Amadou into *kingmaker*. As member of the ARN coalition, he should have given his support to Seyni Oumarou, but he made another U-turn, possibly also because of the negative reaction by Moden members to the alliance with the MNSD. On 9 February, the Moden leader declared his support for Mahamane Issoufou in the presidential run-off, thus creating – together with three lesser parties – a *two-thirds majority* in the National Assembly (78 seats). In August, the PNDS-led majority was boosted to 84, when some minor parties agreed to join what was now called the 'Mouvance pour la Renaissance du Niger'.

In the *presidential run-off* on 12 March, Issoufou took 57.9% of the votes and Seyni Oumarou 42.1%. Turnout was 48%. On 16 March, Oumarou conceded defeat, opening the way for Issoufou's accession to the highest office. Nicknamed 'Zaki' (lion), the 59-year-old mining engineer had twice been runner-up. This experience had had a sobering effect on a man known not only for his leftist convictions (he was active in the Socialist International and is a friend of fellow 'eternal' opposition leader-turned president, Alpha Condé of Guinea) but also for his fierce temper. It was essentially Tandja's ill-judged attempt to hang on to the presidency that paved the way for his success. Issoufou is also one of the few leading politicians without a military background. With the new president sworn in on 7 April, the textbook transition begun with the 'republican' coup of junta leader Salou Djibo the previous year came to an end.

Issoufou appointed Brigi Rafini, a technocrat and Tuareg from the northern town of Iferouâne, as *prime minister* – an appointment calculated to appease Niger's chronically malcontent Tuareg community, while harmlesss for Issoufou as Rafini was not part of his inner circle. Foreign affairs went to Bazoum Mohamed, a member of that inner group; Foumakoye Gado, also a presidential confidant, got the important ministry of energy and mining; and Issoufou's ally, Karidjo Mahamadou, became minister of defence.

Marou Amadou, a human rights campaigner prominent in the struggle against Tandja, became minister of justice. The *cabinet* included five women. In a minor *reshuffle* on 12 September, intended to accommodate the disappointments of the government's Moden partner about their ministerial posts, mining was made into a separate ministry, together with industrial development, and awarded to Hamidou Tchiana, an ally of Hama Amadou. The Moden leader himself had been elected chair of the National Assembly on 19 April, taking over from Mahamane Ousmane. In a break with the past, President Issoufou invited Seyni Oumarou to join a government of national unity, but the MNSD leader declined.

The happy end to the crisis of the previous years went hand in hand with an *ambitious government programme.* Issoufou pledged to work for strong republican institutions and vast investment in agriculture, irrigation, water supply and livestock improvement (the right to education, drinking water and an adequate diet was inscribed in the constitution). The entire five-year development plan would require funds to the tune of € 9 bn, to be supplied by fiscal revenues and development aid and to be undergirded by a projected growth rate of 7%. The agricultural part of Issoufou's plans would be allocated a prospective € 1.8 bn.

In May, the National Assembly passed a bill granting amnesty to the former junta – a sine qua non for a smooth beginning of the '7th Republic'. The *armed forces* had already, on 7 March, signed a republican pact with political parties, the media and civil society groups, vowing to respect the new constitution. In reference to the previous two years, the pact noted that Niger was sick and its consciousness needed to be enhanced with regard to respect for democratic and constitutional principles. However, if the army came out of the transition with its republican reputation reinforced, this did not apply to all sections of the military, for many officers still harboured sympathy for Tandja. On 22 July, several officers were detained on suspicion of plotting to kill the new president. They were said to have conceived a *coup plan* for 16 July, when Issoufou would be assassinated.

Those arrested included a major and a lieutenant, a member of the presidential guard and a captain formerly responsible for the security of Salou Djibo. On 9 September, Colonel Abdoulaye Badié, Salou Djibo's former secretary who had already been detained over similar rumours in October 2010, was re-arrested and another top military man was arrested two days later. It was alleged that the rebellious military were angered by Issoufou's efforts to stamp out corruption, which had led to several dismissals. However, this could hardly be expected to be the end of the matter, as the prospective start of oil production would make the country less dependent on foreign aid and thus less susceptible to the corrective pressure of donors.

On 7 January, a *kidnapping incident* sent shockwaves through Niger's Western community. Members of al-Qaida in the Islamic Maghreb (AQIM) snatched two young Frenchmen from a restaurant in the capital Niamey, 700 m. from the presidential palace. This blatant act was clearly intended to intimidate Niger's Western partners, and the victims – one an NGO worker about to marry a Nigérien girl, the other his friend who had come over for the wedding – were taken towards the border with Mali. The French government, in close consultation with the Niger and Mali authorities, dispatched helicopters from a base in Ouagadougou, while Nigérien gendarmerie pursued the kidnappers on land. One party of gendarmes fell victim to an AQIM ambush (with four taken prisoner), but French special forces caught up with the kidnappers, reportedly just across the border in Mali. Violent clashes took place in which two French military, including one of the helicopter pilots, were wounded. Eight people were killed: four kidnappers, three Nigérien gendarmes and the two hostages, one of whom was executed by the AQIM men, and the other caught in the cross-fire (his body was later found badly burned).

If the swift response was the proper answer to the *AQIM challenge*, the incident did not fail to increase concern over security. US Peace Corps volunteers were withdrawn, and Niamey's security industry received a new boost. Issoufou's government vowed to fight

AQIM and trans-border crime. In late February, three hostages who had been kidnapped from the uranium town of Arlit in September 2010 were released from an AQIM hide-out in Mali: one Togolese, a Malagasy and a French woman sick with cancer; this left four Frenchmen from Arlit in AQIM hands. On 23 March, AQIM demanded a € 90 m ransom. It was unknown whether money had been paid for the freed hostages. In June, 80 km north of Arlit, Niger soldiers clashed with men coming from Libya who were alleged to be on their way to an AQIM hide-out. Their vehicles were carrying explosives and detonators of Czech manufacture. One soldier and one militant were killed and six soldiers wounded. As a result of the crisis in Libya, the armed forces were put on maximum alert. In September, another clash took place in the Agadez region, in which three AQIM militants were killed and arms were recovered, along with 50 young men who were being recruited, either forcibly or with the promise of cash. In comparison, the threat posed by ordinary Tuareg rebels was insignificant. In July, members of former rebel forces surrendered weapons, vehicles and ammunition. Prime Minister Rafini, himself a Tuareg, appealed for the loyalty of his people. Security in the border region with Mali continued to be problematic. In April, 24 pastoralists were killed and several wounded in a cattle camp when armed men from Mali staged an attack.

Issoufou seemed determined to continue the clean-up started by the junta in the wake of Tandja's overthrow. A 'cour des comptes', established in 2010, produced a damning report in March about *financial irregularities* between 1996 and 2009, most of them involving false or inflated procurement invoices. A total of 3,000 people had by now come under scrutiny, and reported embezzlements totalled CFAfr 77 bn. The Ibrahim Index of African governance rated Niger's performance as very poor (ranking 39th out of 53 countries and in sixth place among the eight-member UEMOA). One of Tandja's sons, arrested in 2010, still awaited trial, together with a former mining minister, for corruption involving mining licences.

On 16 January, *former president Tandja* was moved from house arrest to a state prison, having been charged with financial malfeasance (the previous year the ECOWAS court of justice had ruled his detention without charge illegal). However, in May, an appeals court dismissed all charges, arguing that it was constitutionally impossible to try a head of state after he had left office. Although this provided an unsatisfactory conclusion to the clean-up campaign, the law had been designed in this way to prevent politically motivated cases against former leaders. Tandja left jail on 10 May. However, an audience granted by Issoufou to Seyni Oumarou on 12 May was said to mark the end of Tandja's long-standing influence.

The insurrection and regime change taking place in Libya created a huge *refugee crisis*. By April, almost 60,000 sub-Saharan Africans had made their dangerous way across the desert and found themselves in overstretched camps. Most having worked for years in menial jobs in Libya, they found themselves the target of racist and revenge attacks by rebel militias, being accused of connivance with Kadhafi's regime – West African Tuareg fighters had been paid huge sums of money to defend the maverick leader against the rebels. Many Nigériens struggled to receive family members while having to cope with a drop in remittances. By the summer, some 210,000 Nigériens were said to have returned home.

Although the 2010 Human Development Index ranked Niger as the third poorest country in the world (two places higher than in 2009), *social unrest* was limited. On 1 August, police broke up demonstrations in the capital where people were protesting against blackouts due to disruptions in the electricity supplies from Nigeria (the source of 80% of the country's power). Several people were wounded and some were arrested. Top police officials were sacked in the wake of clashes between police and demonstrators in Niger's second city, Zinder, on 6–7 December.

Foreign Affairs

With the return to civilian rule, the country's membership rights in ECOWAS and the AU were restored. At the end of May, Issoufou participated in the Africa outreach session at the G8 summit in Deauville, which signalled continuing close relations with France. Together with three other sub-Saharan heads of state, Issoufou visited the White House on 29 July (a particularly gratifying experience for a politician who had been so long in the wilderness).

Relations with France and the US were expected to remain dominated by *concerns over security*. Cooperation in this area also included West African countries, as well as Algeria. On 20 May, a get-together began in Bamako, involving Niger, Mali, Mauritania and Algeria, to discuss terrorism and trans-border crime. While Mali had called for a regional approach and the training of tens of thousands of troops to tackle the AQIM challenge, Algeria remained lukewarm, despite the fallout of the Libyan crisis (it had consistently opposed the involvement of France in this issue). Nevertheless, Mali and Niger vowed to strengthen their cooperation. This pattern repeated itself on 7–8 September at a meeting in Algiers. The Algerians claimed that Algeria and its West African partners needed to develop their own security capabilities and that foreign troops should be kept out, while Niger warned that the region had been turned into a powder keg. Relations with *Nigeria* were reinforced, strengthening cooperation to counter the threat of terrorism and banditry (AQIM in Niger were reported to have had contacts with the Boko Haram group in the Nigerian city of Maiduguri). On 9 August, the two countries held talks on the issue and vowed to strengthen border patrols.

The government had to tread cautiously with regard to the deteriorating *crisis in Libya*. In July, Issoufou warned against arms proliferation and the risk of fundamentalists taking power in Tripoli. While other West African states were distancing themselves from Kadhafi or had already recognised the rebel-dominated transitional government, Issoufou stressed Niger's neutrality. On 6 September, as the Libyan regime was falling apart, more than 30 members of Kadhafi's inner circle made their way to Niger, together with one of Kadhafi's sons, Saadi, and the government felt compelled to host them on humanitarian grounds. Niger's stance was complicated by:

the fact that the Kadhafi regime had made substantial gifts to the country; the impossibility of patrolling the common border; the violent treatment of Niger migrant workers by anti-Kadhafi forces; and the fallout of the regime change for security and the Tuareg community. Aghaly Alambo, former leader of the rebel 'Mouvement des Nigériens pour la Justice', had taken up residence in Tripoli after he had made his peace with the Tandja government (brokered by Kadhafi). Upon the latter's fall he travelled back to Niger, together with Libyans loyal to the old regime. Things became more sensitive when the US State Department called on Niger to arrest those senior figures who might become the target of international prosecution, and Libya's rebel forces threatened action if Niger helped Kadhafi himself to escape. While Issoufou promised full cooperation with the ICC, to which Niger is a signatory, the government was much relieved when it turned out that the Libyan leader had remained in his country to meet his maker. Earlier, on 27 August, Issoufou recognised Libya's transitional government, ahead of AU policy on this point, obviously to protect Niger's interests.

Socioeconomic Developments

Early in the year, there was a temporary let-up in the previous year's food shortages, themselves caused by the disappointing 2009 harvests. However, rainfall, though it improved in July and August, proved erratic and the autumn harvests were catastrophic, auguring badly for the situation in 2012. Cereal prices began to rise after the harvest, which is unusual, and in December the UN Emergency Response Fund said it would allocate $ 6 m to help people cope with *food shortages*. By then some 750,000 people in various parts of the country were already food insecure, especially as they had not yet recovered from the previous year's difficulties. The 2010 harvest, better than in 2009, had not fully eradicated *malnutrition*, and the overall 2011 harvest was 11% lower than the average of the five preceding years. UNICEF reported on 21 July that more than 15% of children were suffering from acute malnutrition. The civilian government, like the preceding junta, was open about the country's problems (in contrast to the Tandja years). In May, it put the number of people facing severe food shortages at 1.2 m (this was before the autumn harvest!), with another 1.4 m suffering moderate shortages.

Issoufou called for international help. His € 1.8 bn *agricultural programme* aimed to increase production by 7.4% annually, but this target was unlikely to be met in 2011. Government revenue was prioritised to the agricultural and livestock sectors (besides education), which together accounted for nearly 85% of the work force and 40% of GDP. On 24 August, the government launched an irrigation pilot project worth CFAfr 10 bn aimed at the production of 1 m tonnes of various types of food crops (the Kandadji dam on the River Niger was still under construction). The ADF provided a $ 33.8 m grant to finance irrigation projects in the country's central-eastern regions.

Meanwhile, numerous people were leaving for *the cities*, with urban residents hard pressed to assist rural relatives – the refugees coming from Libya did not ease the situation. The capital alone had witnessed a population growth of 6% annually for the five preceding years. Housing projects during the Tandja years had hardly taken off, but the new civilian government committed itself to constructing 1,000 social housing units annually in the north-west of the city during the next five years.

Much-needed *foreign aid* began to flow again. At the beginning of the year, the 'Banque Ouest Africaine de Développement' granted a loan of CFAfr 22 bn for road construction and irrigation projects (and later lent $ 107 m for energy programmes). The OPEC Fund for International Development gave loans totalling more than $ 18 m for road upgrading and rural development. China gave a grant for the extension of the second bridge across the River Niger in the capital. An IDA loan of $ 52 m was to help overcome institutional bottlenecks hindering road maintenance and rural development, among other things. The EU released € 25 m in budget support in July, the first tranche since the accession of Issoufou to the presidency and marking the full resumption of ties. If all went well, € 450 m worth of European aid would be disbursed in the next five years.

Towards year's end, the IMF awarded an ECF facility to the tune of $ 123 m, intended to help in absorbing the fall in remittances and the disappointing harvest. The *World Bank* provided assistance for a social safety net for vulnerable households that should cover 1 m people over five years by way of regular transfers of small amounts of money paid out to women. Health and water were also targeted in the programme, which totalled $ 280 m. In May, the government reduced the national *budget* by 6.6% to cope with delays in aid transfers and various administrative problems. While the overall budget declined, at some CFAfr 65.9 bn, it was expected that the government would still aim to increase spending on food security and the military – the latter in order to confront the country's growing security threats. The 2010 growth figure according to the national statistical agency appeared higher than first expected (7.5% as against ca. 3%). By contrast, optimistic figures for 2011 were later toned down to 3.8% as a result of the catastrophic harvest.

The start of Chinese *uranium* mining at Teguidan Tessoumt (Azélik) at the end of 2010 was followed by the official opening on 17 March. Salou Djibo had already received the vice-president of the China National Nuclear Corporation, which together with a South Korean firm controls two-thirds of the mine's capital (and Niger a blocking one-third). A third of the mine's expected yearly 700 tonnes production (out of a national total of 3,000 tonnes) would be to the benefit of the national budget. Representing around half of the country's exports, the importance of the yellow cake was expected to grow further, despite the nuclear disaster in Japan. Australian, Canadian and Indian firms remained active in exploration. French Areva, which had security for its personnel reinforced after the kidnappings that had taken place in 2010, remained dominant. According to the World Nuclear Association, Niger's uranium production increased in 2010 by 29.4% to 4,198 tonnes, becoming the world's number five.

Oil production also began. Extraction from the Agadem block near the Chadian border started in September. Chinese construction of the 460-km pipeline connecting the block to a refinery in Zinder was also completed. With oil production coming on stream in 2012, growth could rise to 14%, boosting domestic revenue. The refinery could produce 20,000 b/d, destined for the domestic market to ease local consumption (7,000 b/d), although transportation might become a problem. In any case, it could cut the country's import bill. In the meantime, the Chinese would construct another pipeline, probably to link up with the Chadian-Cameroonian one, for the transportation of their 60% share of the crude. Daily total production could grow to 100,000 barrels. However, disagreement arose over the costs of the refinery, which was officially opened on 28 November but whose revenue could possibly not be enough to cover the government's share in its capital outlay, advanced by the Chinese. The China National Petroleum Corporation (CNPC) demanded a higher share of Agadem's output and claimed that the deposed Tandja had agreed to this. Typically for the latter's opaque dealings with Chinese firms, the new minister of finance disputed the existence of such an agreement. NGOs asked the government to review the CNPC contract. On 2 March, Niger was declared compliant with the Extractive Industries Transparency Initiative. The new constitution reserves 15% of revenues in this field for the communities where mining or production takes place.

Niger in 2012

The second year of the 7th republic saw a remarkable degree of stability. The government reinforced its hold on power, and, despite the marginalisation of the opposition, Niger improved its position on democracy indexes. Greater cohesion and a range of government measures went some way towards alleviating social conditions, despite the return of huge numbers of migrant workers from Libya. The country faced security threats from Boko Haram Islamists in north-eastern Nigeria and even more from the northern regions of Mali, where state control collapsed with the influx of heavily armed Tuareg and Islamist fighters into areas bordering on Niger. The government of President Mahamadou Issoufou nevertheless managed to keep the national territory under control, notwithstanding occasional kidnap incidents. Although not guaranteeing an untroubled future, increased security budgets and cautious government policies played a positive role, as did astute manoeuvring by Issoufou, who turned the country into a constructive international partner. The food situation worsened rapidly during the first part of the year. July to October saw the worst floods in decades, but later harvests exceeded immediate needs. Overall economic performance was positive, with record growth anticipated thanks to oil production and higher uranium output. Nevertheless, more than 40% of the population continued to struggle under the poverty datum line.

Domestic Politics

President Mahamadou Issoufou's 'Parti Nigérien pour la Démocratie et le Socialisme' (PNDS) enjoyed a dominant political position. However, since it held less than a third of the seats in parliament, it depended on the support of other parties. It was backed by five of the eight parties represented in the National Assembly,

© KONINKLIJKE BRILL NV, LEIDEN, 2019 | DOI:10.1163/9789004401440_006

particularly important among which was its main *coalition partner*, Moden-Lumana ('Mouvement Démocratique Nigérien'), the party of former prime minister Hama Amadou. It thus commanded a comfortable majority. Observers expected that Issoufou would be careful not to antagonise Hama Amadou, a former presidential candidate, political rival and now chairman of the National Assembly, for fear of pushing Amadou back into the fold of his original political home, the once ruling 'Mouvement National pour la Société du Développement' (MNSD) of deposed former president Tandja, now the principal opposition group and led by Seyni Oumarou.

Nevertheless, Issoufou felt forced to take action in a case of corruption concerning fraudulent election expenses. It involved not only six *opposition* MPs but also two of the presidential majority. Among them was Zakou Djibo, a wealthy Moden member, who resigned in protest on 7 March, thus putting relations between the coalition partners under pressure. The government hesitated to move, but on 2 April the National Assembly voted to lift the immunity of all the MPs involved – although this was against the wishes of the MNSD. The opposition, tainted by the corruption of the Tandja years, had appealed to the Constitutional Court to prevent the vote. It accused Issoufou of violating the separation of powers and threatened to have him prosecuted for perjury. After the Court rejected the case, an MNSD motion of censure was defeated in the Assembly by 84 votes to 29. This paved the way for the vote on the lifting of immunity, which the MNSD boycotted. The outcome underlined the weakening of the opposition; ten former ministers in the Tandja government faced other embezzlement charges. Seyni Oumarou was still a powerful figure, but rumour had it that there was now unrest in the MNSD ranks over his party leadership. Oumarou strengthened his position somewhat by aligning himself with another prominent opposition leader, Mahamane Ousmane (who commanded strong support in the important city of Zinder), but numerous boycotts of parliamentary debates did nothing to improve the MNSD's standing, although elections were not due before 2016.

Issoufou promised that 2012 would be marked by a crusade against *corruption*, which was still a major problem. TI reported that corruption had worsened during the previous year (being classified as 'rampant'). In an indication of how acute conflicts over the issue could become, on 3 January arson destroyed parts of the justice ministry. It was rumoured that the object of the attack was to foil investigations into corruption in the judiciary (a branch of government notorious for its corrupt behaviour). Substantial archival collections going back several decades were lost. Although his anti-graft drive was sure to reinforce his popularity, Issoufou would need to boost judicial capacity in order to make headway in this area, as well as to rein in the inevitable profiteers attached to the new ruling bloc.

Still, the president responded vigorously to corruption in his own ranks. In February, the Constitutional Court declared the allocation of government contracts in certain ministerial departments to be unconstitutional. On 3 April (one day after the Assembly vote lifting the immunity of MPs allegedly involved in graft), Issoufou dismissed the ministers of finance and national supplies/public works – both PNDS stalwarts. The minister of transport, who was involved in another scandal, was similarly replaced. The *cabinet reshuffle* was justified on technical grounds and, if this was less than the whole story, the incoming ministers had professional backgrounds, thus strengthening the image of a government based on merit and ostensibly showing the anti-corruption campaign in a less politicised light.

Besides his many socioeconomic priorities, the president was faced with *increasing security concerns*. Fears were expressed about a link between Malian militants belonging to Al-Qaida in the Islamic Maghreb (AQIM) and Boko Haram in Nigeria. Early in the year, members of Boko Haram were arrested in Diffa, in south-east Niger, while on their way to Mali carrying AQIM contact details and propaganda material, as well as explosives. Considering the impossibility of patrolling every border crossing with Nigeria, one diplomatic source opined that it was only Boko Haram's own decision not to become active in Niger (yet) that accounted for the continued quiet. Although AQIM's influence in Niger remained limited, it did have a small presence in remote areas (although the movement's stronghold was in neighbouring Mali). A kidnap incident involving six African aid workers in the north-central town of Dakoro on 14 October underlined the country's vulnerability – a Chadian aid worker was killed and the other five were released three weeks later, having spent their captivity in Malian territory. The kidnappers were alleged to be members of an AQIM-linked group called the 'Mouvement pour le Tawhîd et le Jihad en Afrique de l'Ouest', whose stronghold was in the Gao region of eastern Mali. As humanitarian agencies shifted non-essential staff to urban hubs, these developments showed that Niger was not immune to the Sahel's worsening security situation. This had already been driven home by the pillaging on 14 September of Zinder's largest Catholic church in response to the infamous anti-Islamic film, 'The Innocence of Muslims'.

Sandwiched between two hotbeds of Islamist activity, Niger's leadership worried about the effect on the country's own malcontent youth. The *defence budget* was increased by 65%, frontier security was beefed up and the armed forces were supplied with new hardware. As the risk of a military coup could never be discounted, Issoufou was said to foster the 'republican'-minded sections of the armed forces. In addition to military measures, Issoufou was aware of the *importance of development*, especially in the northern region. However, though the president's willingness was not in doubt, promises to address the marginalisation of Tuareg communities by providing jobs and facilitating integration into the armed forces were, as ever, slow to materialise. In January, Issoufou organised a 'Forum Paix et Développement' at the uranium town of Arlit, setting out the vision of a multi-year development plan to the tune of CFAfr 1,000 bn (€ 1.5 bn). In October, Prime Minister Rafini, himself a Tuareg from the town of Iferouâne, announced a plan called 'Stratégie de développement et de sécurité dans les zones sahélo-sahariennes du Niger', aimed at preventing spillover from the conflict in Mali. The government promised to cover half the scheme's projected cost of $ 2.5 bn itself, but said it would face difficulties raising the rest, in spite of an EU pledge of $ 118 m.

These measures alone could not have limited the disastrous consequences for Niger of the *coup in Mali* on 22 March, which quickly led to the loss of state control over that country's northern, northeastern and eastern regions, bordering on Niger. The coup went hand in hand with a declaration of independence centred on the cross-border region of Azaouagh by separatist Malian Tuaregs, but they were subsequently defeated by well-armed fighters with a wider, Islamist agenda, many of them returnees from Libya who had fought in Kadhafi's forces. However, despite the influx of Malian refugees in Niger's western region, the collapse of state authority in Mali had by year's end not led to a similar disintegration of control on the Nigérien side of the border.

Several political factors and some basic military facts were relevant here, though they said little about the immediate future. The rebellion in previous years by *Nigérien Tuaregs* united in the 'Mouvement des Nigériens pour la Justice' (MJN) had created numerous victims in the north but had not led to concessions by the government – contrary to the action taken in Mali, Tandja's regime had fought back first and only negotiated afterwards. This meant that many Tuaregs were lukewarm about taking up arms again. Strategically, the Nigérien state had never lost complete control of the all-important Aïr region, the heartland of the uranium riches that also made Niger of greater significance to France than Mali. The government was also careful to disarm Nigérien Tuaregs who returned from Libya (again in contrast to Mali). With the advent of Issoufou's administration, care was taken to involve Tuareg dignitaries in the new dispensation. Besides the appointment as prime minister of Rafini, a relative of the mayor of Iferouâne, where the MJN rebellion started, various figures from the Tuareg community were invited to participate in the new government, gaining positions as adviser to the president or the National Assembly chair, the mayorship of the important northern town of Agadez and seats on the regional council.

However, although these appointments sent out a signal that the government was prepared to involve northern communities in decision-making, many of the posts did not carry real power. Moreover, some of the dignitaries involved had been discredited in the eyes of their own community, as much of the money involved in the Libya-brokered peace of 2009 was said to have ended up in their pockets. In March, Aghaly Ag Alambo, adviser to the Assembly presidency, was detained on suspicion of smuggling arms from Libya, having been mentioned in connection with the transportation of arms from Libya to an AQIM hideout in Mali in June 2011. His arrest proved an embarrassment to Hama Amadou, but also showed that *mistrust* was still rife. Security in the mid-term depended at least in part on whether the situation in Mali would stabilise or deteriorate.

Foreign Affairs

With the advent of Issoufou, the country's *foreign relations improved* substantially. The reopening of USAID's offices in Niger underlined the good relations with the United States – the government being able to benefit from American assistance in counter-terrorism. Relations with France similarly improved (with France's new president, François Hollande, the leaders of both countries now shared a similar ideological outlook). With Issoufou's commitment to development and the requirements of humanitarian relief provision, donors lauded the new government's posture. Development grants and loans to a value of $1 bn were confirmed. Issoufou cleverly used the security threats in the Sahelo-Saharan regions to attract more Western aid. On 13–14 November, a Round Table conference was organised at the Intercontinental Hotel in Paris, where Issoufou received more than 120 foreign representatives to discuss the funding of his development plans. Those present included officials from the AfDB, UEMOA and the Islamic Development Bank, as well as bilateral partners such as France, the UK, Russia, China, Spain and the US. Pledges were made to the tune of $ 4.8 bn – more than had been requested (though this did not amount to even half the projected cost of the government's five-year plan).

Regional security concerns played a role. On 10 August, the EU launched a two-year civilian security mission to reinforce Niger's counter-terrorism and crime-fighting capabilities. To be called EUCAP Sahel Niger, it would entail the dispatch of 50 experts with a budget of € 8.7 m and eventually be expanded to include Mali and Mauritania. Niger was said to be very active in the 'Comité d'état-major opérationnel conjoint' based in the southern Algerian city of Tamanrasset, where Algeria, Mali, Mauritania and Niger collaborated to put the region's security co-operation on a more solid footing.

The conduct of foreign affairs was dominated by the developments in *Mali* and Libya. Niger was one of the more outspoken proponents of a military solution to the disintegration of the Malian state. On 1–2 December, Issoufou received Mali's new president, Dioncounda Traoré, who thanked him for taking in thousands of Malian refugees. Both leaders called for international help in reconquering Mali's northern regions. Exactly how thoroughly the security of the two countries was intertwined was demonstrated on 2 December, when a Malian colonel in Niamey came under attack by unknown assailants. The colonel had fled Mali with 400 Malian military personnel early in May to escape the rebel advance.

Relations with the new regime in *Libya* were difficult, not least because Niger continued to give asylum to one of the sons of Colonel Kadhafi, former football star Saadi. In addition, Bashir Saleh Bashir, Kadhafi's former chief of staff and one of his top aides, was given a diplomatic passport in late 2011 and was said to have been appointed as an adviser to Issoufou. Saleh was born in Agadez and for many years ran Libyan investment funds. (Rumour had it that Issoufou himself owed part of his campaign funds to Kadhafi's generosity.) The attacks in Libya on Nigérien migrant workers in the wake of

Kadhafi's fall and their forced return home continued to impinge on bilateral ties, but when Saadi Kadhafi gave a telephone interview to an Arab news channel on 10 February, predicting another rebellion in Libya, he was put under de facto house arrest and his telephone was cut off. The government still refused to extradite him, as he might face execution. The day after Saadi's interview, armed men raided Niger's embassy in Tripoli, expelling the chargé d'affaires. (The two countries no longer exchanged ambassadors after the fall of Kadhafi.)

Socioeconomic Developments

In the wake of the failed 2011 harvest, the worsening *food crisis* became the primary economic concern. The estimate of the cereal deficit was increased to more than 700,000 tonnes, which meant that 6 m people (ca. one-third of the population) would suffer food shortages. The number of children at risk of severe malnutrition rose to 400,000, compared with 300,000 being treated for malnutrition in 'normal' years. People's ability to cope was significantly weakened by the influx of migrant workers from Libya, whose numbers had swollen by April to 250,000 – most of them men, who in the past had each supported an average of seven people at home and had now lost all their savings. The closure of the border with Nigeria hindered food imports, especially in the (far) east, while Nigériens were prevented from seeking work in Nigeria and sending money to relatives at home. The arrival of 50,000 refugees from Mali made the situation in the west worse. The crisis quickly spread to the cities as a result of galloping food prices and the arrival of destitute people from the countryside. Zinder was hard hit, receiving numerous villagers in search of food, in addition to prostitutes from Nigeria fleeing the violence of Boko Haram.

The government faced the crisis with transparency and timely measures, releasing a total of CFAfr 100 bn (€ 152.4 m) for *emergency*

programmes. Towards the end of January it had already begun selling cereals at subsidised prices and planned for animal fodder and
the purchase of weakened cattle. In June (when shortages began
to peak), it commenced free distribution of food. Although international humanitarian agencies became active early, by April only
40% of $ 229 m in donor aid had been mobilised.

The government also introduced some constructive measures,
including irrigated vegetable cultivation, which led to significantly lower food prices. Baptised '3N' ('les Nigériens Nourrissent les
Nigériens'), the government's agricultural programme aimed to attain food self-sufficiency by way of a five-year plan projected to cost
a total of CFAfr 1,000 bn. The objective was to create a permanent
cereal reserve of 100,000 tonnes. The *agricultural sector* received
CFAfr 100.3 bn in the 2012 budget, compared with CFAfr 21.8 bn in
2011, but the government foresaw a lack of sufficient funding for the
full implementation of the '3N' programme.

During the third quarter, abundant rains led to *massive flooding* in the western region, including Niamey and Dosso – the latter badly affected, with the destruction of 10,000 homes. More than
80 people drowned, and there were outbreaks of cholera (3,854 registered cases) and malaria, as well as an invasion of locusts. More
than half a million people were affected. At least 7,000 fields were
flooded and 120 grain stores destroyed; the western Tillabéri region
lost 42% of its homes. The government announced almost € 1 m in
emergency aid, releasing 1,400 tonnes of cereals, and asked for international assistance. The EU responded with the disbursement of
€ 600,000 emergency funding. As locusts did not arrive till after the
grain ripened, *harvests* overall exceeded demand – auguring well for
2013.

Oil production became a new factor in the economy. The Soraz
refinery in Zinder, owned jointly by the government and the China
National Petroleum Corporation, had begun production late in
2011 and had a potential production capacity nearly three times
Niger's domestic needs, so that the country could in principle

become self-sufficient. In early March, Niger struck an accord with Chad for the construction of a pipeline to connect with the Chadian-Cameroonian pipeline in order to ship out the surplus. Maximum production in Agadem was between 60,000 and 80,000 b/d, and reserves were estimated at a total of 483 m barrels, but construction of the pipelines had not begun by year's end. Moreover, in spite of the completion of a 400 km pipeline connecting Agadem with the Zinder refinery, there were problems. The government set a price for petroleum that could not compete with the subsidised price of Nigerian fuel.

Protests against *fuel prices* erupted, in which two people were killed. On 21 September, the government responded by lowering fuel prices by 6%. Taxi drivers demanded a 30% cut and increased fares by half. New protests took place in Niamey on 21 October, and another 7% cut in fuel prices was foreseen for January 2013. Meanwhile, export to Nigeria of the refined surplus was hindered by its higher price, and Zinder's refinery began to suffer from a lack of storage facilities and distribution problems. Operations had to be discontinued, causing substantial losses, and by year's end the refinery was working at half capacity. Fuel lorry drivers went on strike to protest against delays at the refinery, causing shortages and new price increases in the capital.

Uranium production had its problems, too. In the wake of the Fukushima disaster, prices plummeted by 30%. Areva was facing losses and the government feared that construction of the giant new mine at Imouraren would be endangered. Construction slowed, and the opening of the mine was expected to be delayed. On 25 April, workers at Imouraren went on a week's strike over pay and working conditions and a one-day strike took place at the Somaïr mine in Arlit on 20 August. There were also environmental concerns about the impact of Imouraren. In addition, on 11 May a court judgement in France required Areva to pay € 200,000 in compensation to the family of a Frenchman who had worked at Areva's Akokak mine and had died of lung cancer. A Nigérien NGO demanded that similar compensation be paid to Nigérien workers. At year's end, Areva began a libel suit against an NGO, accusing it of trying to bribe Issoufou with the offer of a plane. Production at its other mine, the Somaïr mine at Arlit, reached record levels, while the new Chinese mine at Azélik increased its production of yellow cake.

Mainly as a consequence of oil production, analysts foresaw *record growth*. Real GDP growth was initially expected to reach 9.4%, according to the Economist Intelligence Unit, and then to fall in 2013 as a result of diminishing capital investment. The IMF thought 13.4% growth was possible (in the autumn it increased its forecast to 14.5%). The IMF also corrected its estimate of the 2011 growth rate upwards to 5.5%. The 2012 figures could decrease, however, as a result of the bottlenecks in oil production.

Much of this was good news for Issoufou's government, which entertained ambitious plans. Investments in education to the tune of CFAfr 1.2 bn were projected over a five-year period. The agricultural sector would receive CFAfr 100.3 bn (a fivefold increase as compared to the previous year), and the overall *budget* was set at CFAfr 1,262 bn. The budget was increased three times as a result of the food and security crises, but the 2013 budget saw only small increases, as administrative capacities, among other things, hindered investment spending. Nevertheless, new *infrastructure projects* got underway, including various road repair and construction plans. France and China announced new aid agreements, as did the IDA, ADF and World Bank. As shown by the World Bank aid, which was partly aimed at the reintegration of returnees from Libya, this could also help offset the negative consequences of the poor relations with the new Libyan government. The Chinese decided to invest in a new sugar refinery. Total FDI was among the highest in UEMOA (reflecting investment in oil and uranium production). Even so, the government was planning to revise its investment code in cooperation with the World Bank; in the latter's Doing Business Report, Niger was among the worst performers in terms of business environment, trailing behind Zimbabwe and Afghanistan.

The government also risked becoming the victim of its *many promises*, however well intentioned. In addition to fuel protests, strikes by magistrates and civil servants took place during the summer as food prices peaked ahead of the cereal harvest. The minimum monthly wage was increased from CFAfr 27,000 to CFAfr 30,047 (€ 45.80). The HDI figures for 2011 showed Niger to be the second least developed country in the world (just ahead of the DRC). Annual per capita income was stalled at $ 641, life expectancy at 54 years, and average schooling for males at 1.4 years – a bleak figure in a country where 85% of the population were under 35. More than 40% were living below the *poverty* datum line of less than $ 1.25 a day. On a positive note, *media freedom* improved substantially. Issoufou, who developed the habit of organising unorchestrated press conferences and taking media representatives on his tours, signed a declaration calling for the decriminalisation of defamation (although four newspapers were sued, mainly as result of unfounded and libellous reporting, a persistent feature in the country's media). There were now 11 television stations (of which nine were private), an increase of seven since 2010, and more than 70 newspaper publications (compared with 50 in 2011).

Niger in 2013

The government charted its way through the minefield of challenges posed by the war between Islamist groups and French-led forces in neighbouring Mali and Boko Haram's revolt in Nigeria. Although Niger was seen by the outside world as a beacon of relative stability, the country's vulnerability showed itself in attacks on a military base and uranium mine by Islamists driven out of Malian territory, as well as in a jail-break in the capital, Niamey, involving Boko Haram fighters. A boost in defence spending was followed by massive troop deployment along the Malian border, the dispatch of soldiers to assist in the French- and Chadian-led reconquest of north-east Mali, and the closure of the border with Nigeria. The attacks in Niger heightened popular anxiety and led to new security measures. In August, the appointment of a government of national unity led to the first political crisis since President Mahamadou Issoufou had taken office in 2011. Defended as a security measure, the reshuffle was part of the manoeuvring between Issoufou and his main coalition partner, National Assembly chair Hama Amadou, ahead of the 2016 presidential polls. Insufficient rainfall further compounded the fragile food supply. Uranium output suffered from the attack on mining installations. With its contract set to expire on 31 December, French nuclear energy group Areva got involved in tense negotiations with the government over the renewal of the agreement. Talks had not been concluded by year's end. Fresh delays in the completion of the hydro-electric Kandadji dam, in addition to the worst power failures in years, exposed the country's rickety infrastructure.

Domestic Politics

While President Issoufou enjoyed a comfortable majority with the backing of five of the Assembly's eight political parties united in the

© KONINKLIJKE BRILL NV, LEIDEN, 2019 | DOI:10.1163/9789004401440_007

'Mouvance pour la Renaissance du Niger' (MRN), he repeatedly expressed his desire for a *government of national unity*. Now presented in the context of national security, the idea was linked to manoeuvres ahead of the presidential elections due in 2016. A national government might be able to discourage the defection from the MRN by the second largest party, the 'Mouvement Démocratique Nigérien' (Moden-Lumana) led by Issoufou's main rival for the presidency, Hama Amadou (also National Assembly chair), and prevent the development of an opposition block from which Amadou could make his bid. The urgency of the need for action imposed itself on Issoufou as Amadou-oriented newspapers began to criticise Issoufou's government, triggering fears that Amadou was preparing a censure motion, the dissolution of the Assembly and early elections. Members of the largest opposition party, the 'Mouvement National pour la Société du Développement' (MNSD), were interested in Issoufou's overtures, but an initial attempt to lure them to the government side came to nothing.

In the end, the *cabinet reshuffle* announced on 13 August led to internal divisions in both the MNSD and Moden. While the Tuareg Prime Minister Brigi Rafini was reappointed and key portfolios remained in the hands of presidential loyalists, six MNSD members entered the cabinet – without their party's permission. On 17 August, Hama Amadou announced the withdrawal of seven of his cabinet ministers, but three of them, including Minister of Mining and Moden Secretary-General Omar Hamidou Tchiana, refused to leave. The country's first government of national unity included no fewer than 35 ministers (of whom only five were women). Of the major departments, only the interior ministry changed hands, but it remained under the control of a presidential loyalist, Massoudou Hassoumi.

If in consequence the presidential majority in the Assembly fell to three, the result for the opposition was worse. While Hama Amadou retained control of the influential Assembly presidency, he had no choice but to join a *reduced opposition block* renamed 'Alliance pour la République, la Démocratie et la Réconciliation'. While Amadou's departure from the governing coalition was not unexpected, observers surmised that he might have moved too soon. With 12 opposition MPs disobeying their party leaderships and supporting the new cabinet, Prime Minister Rafini easily won a vote of confidence on 9–10 November. The reconfigurations did little to change the overall picture of Nigérien politics, which ever since the early 1990s had been marked by poor party discipline and constantly shifting alignments between the same political tycoons.

President Issoufou continued his crusade against *corruption*: 21 health officials accused of stealing some $ 2 m from funds meant for vaccination campaigns were arrested early in the year (and another five followed in May). On 6 May, Foukory Ibrahim, an associate of former president Tandja and an MP for the MNSD, was charged with embezzling more than $ 40 m as head of Nigelec, the state electricity company. Nevertheless, on TI's corruption perception index, Niger jumped from 134th to 113th place, signifying some gains in the battle against corruption.

With the onset of foreign military intervention to fight off Islamist fighters in *northern Mali*, the government resolved to dispatch troops in support of the operations spearheaded by French and Chadian forces. On 16 January, the National Assembly overwhelmingly approved the deployment, which involved some 700 men. In addition, more than 5,000 military personnel were deployed to patrol the porous borders, of whom 500 were stationed at Arlit, the northern town that was the site of several uranium mines. However, even with the army's expansion (to a projected 20,000 in 2014), patrolling the borders proved daunting, especially on the frontier with Libya, to where many of the defeated Islamist forces in Mali escaped. The government increased the salaries paid to key military units, hired new staff for the intelligence services, placed informers in strategic villages and tried to seal the eastern two-thirds of the frontier with Nigeria in an attempt to prevent a spill over of violence by Boko Haram. *Security expenditure* now totalled 10% of the national budget, for which some $ 80 m was diverted from spending on education and health.

With resources stretched, foreign partners provided *substantial military aid*. Dozens of French special forces personnel were sent to protect uranium mines in Arlit, some 100 French troops were stationed in the capital, and the government signed an agreement with the US for the establishment of an American base near the northern desert town of Agadez to accommodate a maximum of 300 men. In addition to providing training, the French donated three Gazelle helicopters with 20 mm cannon. In April, the government purchased two Sukhoi jet fighters manned by Ukrainians, a huge expense but the pride of the armed forces. In February, four drones were stationed at a base near Niamey, manned by American and French personnel, for surveillance of the war zones in Mali. The government had wanted them to be armed but the US feared that this could create a backlash. Indeed, civil society groups aired criticism about the stationing of French troops in Arlit and the ICG warned that the government was involving itself in security strategies over which it exercised little influence.

Thus, while the war in Mali posed an extreme danger to national security, the government took some risk with regard to the *popular response*. With many Tuareg youths distrustful of uniformed officials, some might be susceptible to recruitment by Islamist groups. Despite the involvement of Tuareg dignitaries at the highest level of the political system, overall Tuaregs enjoyed little real representation in the capital. Prime Minister Rafini nevertheless assured journalists that Niger's peoples were cooperating with the authorities. Indeed, well-informed observers thought that neither the Islamist 'Mouvement pour l'Unicité et le Jihad en Afrique de l'Ouest' (MUJAO) nor al-Qaida in the Islamic Maghreb (AQIM) had much support among communities in northern Niger, for which the ill-fated Tuareg rebellion of 2007–9 could be partly blamed.

On 23 May, Niger experienced the first *suicide attacks* in its history. In a coordinated twin operation, cars packed with explosives drove into the Somaïr uranium mine in Arlit and a military barracks in Agadez, killing one person at the mine and 24 or 25 on the base. At least a dozen people were wounded and the blast caused extensive damage to the uranium grinding machine – which halted the production of yellow cake. Ten attackers died and French and Nigérien forces needed 24 hours to neutralise the remaining assailants. Responsibility was claimed by both MUJAO and the Algerian leader of Islamist fighters, Mokhtar Belmokhtar, who had distanced himself from the AQIM leadership to form his own jihadist outfit. In fact, he seemed to work closely with MUJAO, with which he formed a new group a couple of months later. Following these attacks, the bloodiest on Niger to date, Issoufou decreed three days of mourning, and in an act of national solidarity visited Agadez and Arlit in the company of the leader of the opposition and Assembly chair Hama Amadou. The attackers seemed to have come from southern Libya (from where it would have been one night's ride to the targets).

In June, *new attacks* took place – this time right in the capital. On 1 June, assailants attacked the prison in Niamey to free 22 Islamists, including Cheibane Ould Hama, a Malian who was serving a jail term for the murder of several Saudi citizens in 2009 (in 2000 he had murdered a US diplomat in Niamey). The attack was probably undertaken by North African MUJAO fighters after three Boko Haram inmates killed several guards with pistols smuggled into the facility; just two months previously Nigérien forces had participated in a raid with Nigerian troops on a Boko Haram hideout in north-eastern Nigeria. The prison governor and another official were arrested and the three Boko Haram fighters recaptured (with the death of one of them), while French forces, tipped off by Nigérien intelligence, re-arrested Cheibane in north-eastern Mali on 26 November. On 11 June, assailants attacked a gendarmerie base on the outskirts of the capital but were driven away. These attacks, coupled with power failures that plunged Niamey into darkness for several weeks, created general anxiety. With increased security measures in place, which seriously affected traffic, the capital seemed in a state of siege. In early September, army troops clashed with drugs traffickers in the Mangueni-Djado region. Though they may have been simply Tubus going about their business, this zone was also frequented by Islamist fighters on their way to and from their Libyan sanctuary.

29 October saw the release of the 'Arlit four' – French workers kidnapped from a uranium mine at Arlit three years earlier and held by men loyal to Abou Zeid, the Algerian AQIM leader killed in Mali by French and Chadian forces on 25 February. Since the kidnappers' political demands had not been met, nor any detained fighters released, rumours of payment of a ransom to the tune of € 20–25 m quickly hit the headlines. The French military were said to be furious, as any such payments would allow Islamist groups to replenish their resources. An American report on the Sahel's *kidnapping industry* had it that AQIM had acquired more than $ 100 m since 2003 (special bank accounts having been opened in Mauritania for the purpose). The money for the Arlit hostages may have come from secret French state funds or from Areva, in which the French state holds an 80% stake. The French government, which had been under constant pressure to help in the liberation of the hostages, denied paying any money, but the defence minister was known to have made several trips to Niamey. Issoufou was said to have played a key role in the process, appointing Mohamed Akotey, chairman of Areva's new uranium mine at Imouraren, as mediator: a Tuareg with family connections in north-eastern Mali, he made contact with the kidnappers. The Islamists' partial dislocation in the war against French and Chadian forces undoubtedly facilitated the deal. Observers also speculated that Issoufou's role could become a quid pro quo in the negotiations on the renewal of Areva's mining contract.

Foreign Affairs

Ties with *France* received a boost as a result of Niger's key geostrategic role in the war in Mali, its perceived relative stability in the troubled Sahelian region and the threats posed by Islamist fighters to the country's security. Issoufou visited French President François Hollande four times – his last visit on 5–7 December being in the context of a summit conference on peace and security in Africa. The meeting was partly overshadowed by the difficult negotiations with Areva. Issoufou, a mining engineer himself, went on record pleading for greater equilibrium in relations with the French nuclear consortium. French Foreign Minister Laurent Fabius visited Niger in the wake of the double suicide mission on 23 May.

By contrast, these attacks led to a worsening of relations with *Libya* – already poor since the fall of Kadhafi – because of strong suspicions that the attackers had staged their operations from south-west Libya. This suspicion was also voiced by France's foreign minister, who urged cooperation between Libya and the Sahelian countries. Issoufou's statement that the attackers had come from the Fezzan drew an angry if unpersuasive denial from the Libyans, who still had an axe to grind with Niger over its refusal to extradite one of Kadhafi's sons, former football star Saadi (because of fear that he might not get a fair trial). Libya reiterated its call for Saadi's extradition and towards the end of May expelled more than 1,000 West African workers, the majority of whom were Nigériens. Suffering hunger and thirst in the course of their summary deportation, two deportees were alleged to have died. Most lost all their savings. Niger refused to budge and actually became convinced that the suicide attacks had been planned in Derna, in north-east Libya (and also outside the control of the 'central government' in Tripoli). The Nigériens aspired to discuss joint border patrols, but the messy post-Kadhafi situation obstructed normal diplomatic contacts.

Relations with Niger's Sahelian neighbours remained good, buttressed by the shared Islamist challenges to their security (in the case of Chad, Mali and Nigeria) and the signing of a new military cooperation agreement with Mauritania on 20 August. Ties with *Burkina Faso* received a boost when the International Court of Justice in The Hague issued its ruling on a simmering border conflict. The disputed territory involved was more or less carved in two, the northern half going to Niger, with the proviso that both countries should take into account the needs of their nomadic populations when arranging the details of border control. Both countries expressed satisfaction with the ruling, which would end confusion about border patrols and tax collection. (This state of affairs dated back to colonial times, when the territory of Burkina Faso, formerly Upper Volta, had been temporarily suppressed by the French and shared out between neighbouring colonies.) Gold reserves in the border zone made the need for a settlement more urgent.

Socioeconomic Developments

The rainy season ended prematurely, impeding the ripening of cereal crops. This, combined with attacks by locusts and caterpillars, led to *seriously deficient harvests*, and the government soon had to subsidise food. As early as February, well before the annual harvest, the government launched the so-called 2013 Global Call for humanitarian aid to the tune of CFAfr 177 bn. While the 2012 harvest had been 27% above average, the country was still recovering from the catastrophic 2011 crop and destructive floods the following year. Thus, an estimated 3 m people were in need of assistance. The regions of Zinder, Tahoua and Tillabéri were worst affected. In the province of Diffa, food production suffered as farmers fled the Nigerian part of the Lake Chad area, which was engulfed in the war against Boko Haram. The hostilities negatively impacted on this source of additional food imports and also led to the influx of some 6,000 Nigerian refugees, which put further pressure on resources. In the first quarter, cereal prices rose by a third to their highest level in five years.

While the two *uranium* mines, Somaïr and the smaller Cominak, run by Areva at Arlit, had registered record output the previous year (together accounting for one-third of Areva's global yellow cake production), it took the company two months to get production back to normal after the destruction of its grinder at Somaïr. In March, the French consortium announced a contribution of € 35 m to help the government protect its industrial operations. Some observers suggested that this was meant as compensation for the delays in starting up Areva's open pit mine at Imouraren, which would become Africa's largest (producing 5,000 tonnes a year), but whose completion kept being pushed forward. Insecurity was likely to lead to new delays. An Australian uranium company discontinued operations after the attack on Somaïr. Moreover, Western concern over nuclear safety since the Fukushima disaster was still reducing global demand, with spot market prices having plummeted from € 187 to around € 50 a kilo.

Negotiations on the renewal of *Areva's contract* were a protracted balancing act. Fenced in between security threats, an uncertain market and the need to protect export value, the government had to tread carefully. In order to put pressure on the consortium, it mobilised popular support. On 5 April, around 2,000 students marched through the capital denouncing Areva's 'neo-colonialism' and demanding a bigger slice of the revenues from the mines (the government holds 36% and 31% in Somaïr and Cominak, respectively). A bigger demonstration was held in Arlit on 12 October, with allegations being aired about radioactive pollution, and this was followed on 21 December by another march in the capital. Areva threatened to discontinue its operations and the French media reported that it had decided to stop work at the mines owing to diminishing profitability. This was disputed by the government, which on 20 September had announced an independent audit of the mines. Issoufou's administration, which had to make sure that it was seen to fight for a better deal, demanded a more balanced partnership and Areva investment in the country's wider infrastructure. Uranium-derived income represented only 5% of the government budget. Niger argued that this should be raised to at least 20%. On its part, Areva claimed that its two mines could not afford to lose their fiscal privileges. A war of statistics was unleashed in which Areva asserted that

70%–80 % of direct mining revenues (taxes, royalties, dividends and licence fees) landed in state coffers. These figures were difficult to verify. A report by Oxfam claiming that only 13% of direct revenues went to Niger was grossly distorted – it arrived at that figure by ignoring the company's exploitation costs. Set against the background of a 40-year relationship, the bitterness created by this discussion was unprecedented. Both sides refused to budge and at year's end no deal had been struck.

After the logistical difficulties of the previous year, *oil* production picked up. In the first half of the year, output rose by roughly a third compared with 2012 (16,500 b/d). However, construction of the pipeline to link the Agadem production field in the east with the Chadian-Cameroonian pipeline had not started. Although there were concerns over the impact of the May suicide attacks on investment, Niger was still considered an attractive investment target owing to its mineral resources (uranium, oil, coal and gold). In recent years, capital inflows accounted for 30% of all FDI in UEMOA.

However, building on the Kandadji hydro-electric dam ran into difficulties, despite the fact that the World Bank had arranged a $ 203 m loan to start up the second phase of construction. The project, totalling around $ 750 m, would increase *power generation* capacity to 130 MW (from the current 105 MW) and irrigated agriculture to around 55,000 ha. Completion was said to be delayed till 2017, and in July the government terminated its contract with a Russian company active on the site, citing the delays already incurred. Not all the problems were the company's fault, however, as issues such as compensation for the affected population, financial constraints and red tape all played a part. The consequences were immediately made clear when the capital was plunged into darkness for weeks in May, after storms had brought down pylons supporting a power line importing electricity from Nigeria – a considerable part of the power needs of the cities of Dosso, Tillabéri and Niamey depended on these imports. Turbines at a power plant in Niamey broke down under the pressure of demand. The government initiated plans for the building of new plants in Niamey and Tahoua, to be fired by diesel and Nigérien coal, but these would not start operating before 2015 and 2017, respectively. China provided a $ 56 m loan for the construction of two new power lines connecting the oil refinery of Zinder to cities in the eastern and central regions.

Various infrastructural development projects began to take shape, including ambitious plans for *railways* to connect landlocked Niger with Benin and Côte d'Ivoire. For the first railway project, which had been on the books since independence, Niger, Benin and French commercial conglomerate Bolloré established a joint stock company in November with a capital outlay of € 650 m. Upon completion of the section of the railway between Parakou in Benin and Niamey, officially planned for 2015, uranium could be transported from Niger by train to the sea port of Cotonou. The other project was for a railway line to Ouagadougou, Burkina Faso, and Abidjan, Côte d'Ivoire, with completion set for 2021. In both cases, the effect would be a significant reduction in transport costs.

Social tension in the Diffa region led to clashes with security forces on 27 April, in which three protesters sustained bullet wounds. The protests were against limited recruitment in the oil industry and low salaries. Prime Minister Rafini hurried to the region to calm tempers. In February and late March, workers had laid down their tools at the Chinese-run uranium mine near Azélik and had managed to secure a 15% pay increase (which was unlikely to significantly address the wide salary gap between Chinese and local workers – the cause of considerable tension). *Refugees*, as well as *deportees* from Libya, put further pressure on local resources. The number of refugees from Mali rose to at least 60,000. Shockingly, in October the bodies of around 90 people were found in the Sahara near the Algerian border. They had died of thirst after their vehicles had broken down. They appeared to be illegal *migrants* on their way to Algeria, many of them Nigerians and Nigériens from the Magaria region; according to the UN, some 80,000 migrants cross Niger through the desert every year. On 17 November, the government announced that it had broken up the trafficking ring responsible.

It was reported that the mortality rate for *children* under five had been reduced from 326 per 1,000 in 1990 to 114 in 2012. UNICEF, however, reported on 16 October that in the past year alone around 2,500 children had died of malnutrition. Other grim statistics concerned the position of *girls*. Population Minister Maikibi Kadidiatou reported on 11 July that around 75% of girls got married before the age of 18. The government therefore continued to pursue its policy of widening access to reproductive health facilities. One specific bottleneck involved *education*. In 2011, the primary enrolment rate for boys was 84.9% and for girls 67.3%.

Guitarist 'Bombino' (Omara Moctar), a Nigérien Tuareg and a star in his own country, gave a concert for peace called 'Le chant des dunes' on 5 April in Niamey. Two members of his band had died in the repression of the last Tuareg rebellion in 2007, and so his message of peace and solidarity was a rare glimmer of hope.

Niger in 2014

Politics remained conflict-ridden and subject to unpredictable changes in political alliances. Thus, the 2013 rupture between President Mahamadou Issoufou and National Assembly chair Hama Amadou led to a complete disintegration of their relationship in the run-up to the 2016 presidential challenge. Ultimately, Issoufou came out of this conflict as the stronger party as Amadou lost his Assembly presidency and appeared to be heading for the political wilderness. The government put the heat on opposition elements, and the country's image was tarnished by demonstration bans, attacks on politicians' residences and arrests of opposition supporters. By year's end, the situation had calmed down. The realignment of forces led to a rapprochement between Issoufou and Mamadou Tandja (the former president who had been overthrown by the military in February 2010 after refusing to step down after two terms in office). This had the potential to permanently incorporate elements of Tandja's divided party, the 'Mouvement National pour la Société de Développement' (MNSD), into Issoufou's camp. Negotiations with French nuclear energy group Areva on a new uranium contract finally led to an agreement that largely met government demands. This reinforced the domestic standing of the president, who also boosted his international reputation as a key partner in the regional battle against Sahel jihadists. There were a couple of attacks on Nigérien targets, which must be seen as spill-over effects from the Malian theatre. Concern rose over the worsening violence of Nigeria's Boko Haram. Rains led to flooding but stopped prematurely. As in the previous year, this resulted in a deficient cereal harvest.

© KONINKLIJKE BRILL NV, LEIDEN, 2019 | DOI:10.1163/9789004401440_008

Domestic Politics

In an interview on 18 December, the president claimed success in the '3N' programme ('les Nigériens nourissent les Nigériens') to boost agricultural production. He also asserted overachievement in job creation targets and pointed to the new Areva contract, whose increased proceeds could help him to keep his promises in the social and infrastructural domains. Towering over his neutralised rivals, Issoufou declined to speak out on his candidature for the 2016 presidential elections.

This self-confidence came after a turbulent political year that had begun with a peaceful opposition march in the capital Niamey in late December 2013. Organised by the opposition coalition 'Alliance pour la Réconciliation, la Démocratie et la République' (ARDR), this first protest against Issoufou's administration denounced the government's authoritarianism (the previous month it had issued a ban on *opposition marches* – pointing to jihadist threats to national security – although a court later lifted the ban). The rally was attended by MNSD leader Seyni Oumarou and Mahamane Ousmane, leader of the smaller opposition 'Convention Démocratique et Sociale' (CDS). On 5 January, NGOs organised protests in the northern town of Agadez, demanding jobs and better services. Taken by surprise, the government responded on 27 January by arresting several journalists and activists, who were charged with insulting the president and threatening state security. On 8 February, the coalition of government parties staged a counter-rally in Niamey in support of the administration.

The *political climate deteriorated* further when students rioted against grant payment delays (20–21 May), leading to dozens of injuries and arrests. The government claimed the protests had been instigated by Hama Amadou's party, the 'Mouvement Démocratique Nigérien' (Moden-Lumana). On the first day of the protests, assailants shot at the house of Ben Omar Mohamed, 4th vice president of the Assembly and member of one of the lesser parties in the government coalition. There were no casualties. Three days later, the offices of Issoufou's 'Parti Nigérien pour la Démocratie et le Socialisme' (PNDS) were attacked; three people were injured, one of them seriously. Police arrested some 40 Moden members on suspicion of destabilising the country and working towards an army coup d'état. Among those arrested was Hama Amadou's son.

A planned ARDR march was banned, and a coalition of NGOS called 'Collectif Sauvons le Niger' accused the government of *abusing its power*. On 3 June, police released the majority of detainees, including Amadou's son and one of his cabinet staff. Six people were kept in detention on charges of threatening state security, including two former cabinet ministers and the former mayor of Niamey. All were Moden members close to Amadou, still widely seen as Issoufou's main rival in the 2016 polls. Whatever the veracity of the charges, Amadou claimed that the arrests had been orchestrated against his party and that he had been the victim of a poison attempt. On 15 June, the opposition responded with a big rally in the capital. All the principal opposition leaders (Amadou, Oumarou and Ousmane) took part. A rally planned in Niger's second city, Zinder, on 27 June was broken up by police.

These displays of organised discontent and authoritarian reflexes formed the backdrop to a strategy of confrontation. The urgency of a *showdown* became obvious when Amadou increasingly used the Assembly presidency to taunt Issoufou's administration. Secure in his parliamentary immunity (not unimportant in a political system where fallen leaders have frequently been imprisoned), he began to bring accusations of misdemeanours, not all of them convincing, against the government. Early in the year, the government began to take counter-measures, such as effecting changes in Amadou's security retinue. Amadou, who had not spoken to the president since he led Moden's partial departure from the government the previous year, claimed his house was shot at on 16–17 February; the interior minister denied an attack had taken place. Since the government did not command the two-thirds majority needed to depose Amadou, other steps seemed necessary – incongruous ones, yet frequently resorted to in Niger's political arena.

With the physical attacks on a government politician and the PNDS headquarters, the opposition overstepped the mark. The government struck back in late June, mentioning one of Amadou's wives in a baby-trafficking scandal. This involved women in Nigeria giving birth in a 'baby factory' and their off-spring being sold to childless couples in Niger and Benin. Seventeen people were arrested, including Amadou's wife, who was said to have played a central role but denied the charges. On 26 August, the government sought the Assembly's permission for Amadou to be questioned, whereupon the latter secretly left the country for France. The next day, a parliamentary committee decided to *lift* the *chairman's immunity*, an act sanctioned by the Constitutional Court in early September; later that month, an arrest warrant was issued. Amadou claimed the affair was politically motivated and gave fear of assassination as the reason for his flight. The existence of the trafficking ring appeared to be true, however. Among those arrested was Agriculture Minister Abdou Labo. It was widely speculated that Labo, a close ally of Issoufou but a member of the CDS, was sacrificed to counter charges of political motivation.

With Amadou out of the way, Issoufou's electoral prospects improved, though the longer-term consequences of Amadou's political elimination were unclear. As the Moden party was divided between pro- and anti-government wings, Issoufou had little to fear from them, and he faced no threat either from the *new Assembly president*, Amadou Salifou, an MNSD member who the previous year had broken with his party leader, Oumarou, and joined the government majority.

Salifou's election provided Issoufou with an opportunity to drive a bigger wedge into the ranks of the MNSD. Against this background, a *rapprochement* took place between *Issoufou* and the deposed Mamadou *Tandja*, who still played an important role in MNSD affairs. The previous year, Tandja had given his blessing to MNSD secretary-general Albadé Abouba to participate in government – leaving MNSD president Oumarou out in the cold. In a get-together with MNSD supporters in October 2013, Tandja was overheard saying that, when he was deposed from power in 2010, there had been some CFAfr 400 bn in the state's coffers – an amount that could not be accounted for and led opposition elements to accuse Issoufou's administration and the preceding military transition regime (2010–11) of graft. The government, however, used this to put pressure on Tandja. On 26 June, the Supreme Court lifted his ex-presidential immunity, and used this threat to conclude an entente with the man who had dominated Nigérien politics during the previous decade. On 2 July, Issoufou received Tandja at the palace and on 13 November the ex-president, sick with cancer, was flown to Morocco in the new presidential jet for treatment.

Although the courts were still able to restrict government encroachment on *civil liberties*, the administration's actions broke with the enlightenment of the preceding years: one of the worst offenders with regard to media freedom, Issoufou had made Niger an example by becoming the first head of state to sign the 2007 Table Mountain declaration calling for the decriminalisation of defamation in Africa laws.

With the stepping up of attacks in border areas, Niger recorded a first confrontation with *Boko Haram* fighters. An army patrol was ambushed 20 km from the eastern city of Diffa in the first week of May. Several people were wounded and 14 suspects apprehended. Earlier, in February, 20 people in Diffa, where youths had joined Boko Haram mainly for financial gain, were arrested on suspicion of planning attacks across Niger; they were all of Nigerian origin. In Zinder, too, militants were arrested with bomb-making material for an attack on local markets; they were said to have planned to kidnap the governor to press for the release of fellow fighters. The government continued its cautious policy of surveillance and patrols of the porous frontiers without engaging militants across the border unless they were attacked. However, in early November

Boko Haram took control of the Nigerian border town of Malam Fatori, causing Nigerian soldiers to flee across the border into Niger. Military personnel from Chad and Niger, part of a Multinational Joint Task Force established in the 1990s to combat arms smuggling, had also been involved in the fighting, and Niger pulled back some of its men. No further incursions into Nigérien territory took place, but this seemed essentially due to Boko Haram prioritising attacks elsewhere.

The number of *Nigerian refugees* entering Niger increased dramatically. After an attack on the Nigerian village of Gashkar on 16 January, the Nigérien border town of Gueskérou took in 7,000 people who crossed the Komadougou-Yobé River (the frontier between the two countries). In August, some 10,000 refugees crossed into Niger, and in October–November a further 30,000. The total number rose to 100,000 by year's end. On 24 November, Boko Haram attacked the Nigerian border village of Damasak and 3,000 villagers crossed the Komadougou. UNHCR was asked to establish reception centres, 50 km from the border, as local absorption capacity had reached its limit. On 12 December, the government appealed to the international community for help.

On 30 October, men said to belong to the 'Mouvement pour l'Unicité et le Jihad en Afrique de l'Ouest' (MUJAO) in *Mali* launched simultaneous attacks on Malian refugees 60 km from the border, the prison at Ouallam, and a military patrol in Bani Bangou. The government reported that nine soldiers and policemen were killed, along with two of the assailants and one innocent civilian. Ninety of the 118 detainees in the Ouallam prison escaped and fours assailants were captured. On 19 November, another MUJAO attack took place in Bani Bangou, with assailants cutting telephone lines, killing a non-commissioned officer and wounding two. Some of the captured assailants were ethnic Peuls. In the past, several had joined 'Gandakoye' vigilante groups in Mali targeting Tuaregs in acts of ethnic cleansing; in previous years, they had flocked to MUJAO in an effort to get even with Tuaregs pursuing a separatist agenda.

The government played a constructive role in the release of the last French hostage in the hands of al-Qaida in the Islamic Maghreb (AQIM), on 9 December. As a quid pro quo, four AQIM detainees in Bamako, including two of the kidnappers, were released. It seems likely that money was also exchanged, although Issoufou officially denied any knowledge of a ransom payment.

The *defence* budget was set at $ 150–200 m (out of a total budget of $ 3.8 bn) – a fourfold increase over four years. While social expenditure had increased significantly, Foreign Minister Mohamed Bazoum admitted that revenue streams originally budgeted for education and social services had been diverted to the security budget. On 22 October, the government announced the purchase of a reconnaissance plane valued at $ 10.5 m, which was supposed to limit dependence on French and American intelligence gathering. On 20 October, a US drone crashed at Niamey airport for unknown reasons. Ten days earlier, French troops launched a raid against vehicles carrying arms from southern Libya to Mali via the Salvador mountain pass in Niger. French troops established themselves at a desert base in Madama, a colonial fort guarding the border with Libya. The French intended to establish a military presence stretching from Tessalit in northern Mali to Faya-Largeau in Chad. This would enable them to monitor armed elements in the desert, including south-west Libya. France's presence in the Sahara-Sahel was projected to be increased to 3,000 troops, around 1,000 of them to be stationed in Niger. The future headquarters would be in the Chadian capital N'Djaména.

Foreign Affairs

Niger's role in resisting Islamist forces, in addition to facilitating the release of Western hostages, reinforced Issoufou's international position, notwithstanding his government's violations of civil liberties earlier in the year. He toured *Europe* early in April, attended the

4th EU-Africa summit, spoke at the European Parliament and participated in a donor conference for the CBLT, currently under his presidency, in Bologna (Italy).

Relations with *France* were still under pressure resulting from negotiations on Areva's mining contract but improved after the conclusion of a new deal, confirmed by the signing in July of six agreements in various development sectors worth some € 74 m. On his first African tour, new French Prime Minister Manuel Valls visited Niger on 23 November, when he had talks with President Issoufou, met Areva officials and called on the French air base in Niamey.

The USA also enjoyed good relations with Niamey, given Niger's geostrategic importance for American military operations in the Sahel. Operation Flintlock, a US-led annual military exercise in West Africa focusing on anti-terrorist activity, took place in Niger (19 February–9 March). Around 1,000 men from 18 African and European countries participated in the joint operations in the regions of Agadez, Tahoua and Diffa. As a consequence, American Air Force personnel increased in number to 200 men over the year. On 7 August, Issoufou received US Under-Secretary for Defence, Robert Work, and the commander of Africom, General Rodriguez. They agreed to establish a second base for unarmed intelligence drones, in Agadez.

The government decided to extradite associates of the former Kadhafi regime to *Libya*, including a son of Muammar Kadhafi, Saadi. Niger had initially refused to deport him on the grounds that he could face the death penalty. Niger had had good ties with Col. Kadhafi, whose mediation in conflicts with Tuareg communities had afforded him an important role in Nigérien affairs. Ex-military from the Kadhafi regime could move freely in Niamey and enjoyed free telecommunications access – thus angering Libya's official central government. With south-west Libya turned into a launch pad for operations by jihadist fighters, Niger felt forced to change tack. This was made easier when the Kadhafi men were suspected of subversive operations in the Sebha region (on 6 May, six Nigérien migrants were killed there by militias). In late January, Issoufou's government handed over 16 Kadhafi officials, and on 6 March it returned Saadi Kadhafi to the Libyan authorities. As the chaos in Libya escalated, Niger called for Western intervention. On 5 February, Niger's Interior Minister Massoudou Hassoumi reminded Washington and Paris of their responsibility for Libya's current situation. On 13–14 July, the foreign ministers of Libya's neighbours, including Niger's, met in Tunisia to discuss the flow of arms and fighters coming out of Libya, and on 18 December Issoufou reiterated the call for Western intervention. Obviously, this caused new anger in Tripoli.

In mid-February, the *Sahelian countries* (Chad, Niger, Mali, Mauritania and Burkina) agreed to establish a regional security network called 'G5 du Sahel', with its nerve-centre in the Mauritanian capital, Nouakchott. Niger would provide its secretariat. This was followed by another summit in Mauritania in late December, which Issoufou attended.

On 17 May, the president participated in a summit in Paris to discuss *Boko Haram's regional implications*. A ministerial meeting on the same topic in London on 12 June followed. The foreign ministers of Niger, Nigeria, Chad, Benin and Cameroon agreed to set up a Regional Intelligence Fusion Unit. This would involve joint patrols for which each country would provide a batallion. Much of this discussion took place within the framework of the CBLT. On 17–18 March, its defence members met in Yaoundé (Cameroon) to discuss the regional force. A summit meeting in Niamey on 6–7 October, to which Benin was also invited, elaborated the details, announcing that the force would be deployed in November. However, the troops involved in the battle over Malam Fatori in November were part of the Multinational Joint Task Force, which was established by Nigeria in 1994 to combat banditry and in 1998 saw the inclusion of contingents from Chad and Niger. In contrast to Niger, Nigeria did not allow neighbouring armies to cross the border in pursuit of Boko Haram fighters. Issoufou used the Boko Haram crisis to press donors for development funds, in this case pointing to the social implications of the ecological deterioration of the Lake Chad basin.

Socioeconomic Developments

At the end of the year, the government set its *growth* forecast at 5.6%. The IMF thought 6.3% more likely. The 2013 growth rate was retrospectively adjusted down to 4.1%.

In view of the previous year's cereal deficit (estimated at 343,566 tonnes, i.e. 9% of total consumption), *food provision* became an issue of concern. WFP warned that around 2 m people faced severe food shortages and USAID's early warning network showed that several areas – including Tillabéri in the west and Zinder and Diffa in the east – were suffering 'food stress'. Some 23% of the population were estimated to be at risk of severe hunger. Malnutrition among children remained widespread and admission to nutritional recovery centres increased sharply. Donors were asked for $ 80 m in assistance. The government began to sell cereals at subsidised prices early. The failure of the government to feed its population once more led to criticism of Issoufou's much-acclaimed '3N' agricultural policy. However, some claimed that the policy at least lessened famine. The rains stopped prematurely, thus leading to deficient cereal harvests. In August and September, large parts of the country were flooded, affecting more than 50,000 people.

During the negotiations for a new *uranium mining contract*, Niger asked Areva to conform to the mining code of 2006. This meant an increase in royalties from 5.5% to 9–12%. The government further insisted on the lifting of several tax exemptions and for more contributions to the country's infrastructure. On 1 February, Areva resumed production (which had been suspended one month earlier). On 6 February, hundreds of people took to the streets of Niamey to protest against Areva's perceived violation of national laws. Shortly thereafter, the French development minister told the National

Assembly in Paris that Niger's demands were 'legitimate'. On 26 May, the new mining contract was signed. The company committed itself to the 2006 mining code, raising royalties to 12–15% (depending on profits), which it was estimated would bring an additional € 30–35 m into state coffers. Areva would hire Nigériens to head its two mines, build a new headquarters in Niamey and provide $ 123 m for renovation of the 'route de l'uranium', the motorway built for the evacuation of yellow cake to the port of Cotonou in Benin. Niger accepted further delays in the opening of the Imouraren mine, which would be good for 5,000 tonnes of yellow cake and make it the world's second largest uranium producer; the negative impact on uranium prices of the disaster at the Fukushima nuclear reactor in Japan in 2011 still prevented a viable operation.

On 27 June, the president launched the construction of a 600 MW coal power plant north-west of Tahoua. The project, funded by a US company, included coal mining operations and the generation of electricity on a site covering 30 km². It was intended to ameliorate the perennial power shortages, reduce logging for fire wood and combat desertification. Another important development in the field of *infrastructure* concerned the extension of the Cotonou railway. On 8 April, Issoufou, in the presence of his counterparts from Benin and Togo, formally launched the project, which would link Niamey with the Parakou-Cotonou railway in Benin, a dream project since independence. Niger selected the French Bolloré firm as strategic partner; 80% of Niger's freight is exported through the port of Cotonou, transported over derelict roads. Orange-Niger signed a deal with the US firm Intelsat for the use of broadband capacity to extend its mobile phone network further into rural areas. Celtel was given a licence to develop a 3G network (July–August). Niger had some 7 m mobile phone subscribers in 2013. Finally, the country purchased a new presidential jet, a € 30 m Boeing 737. This was criticised by the opposition and civil society groups. Pilots said the old plane, which had been built in the 1970s, was no longer safe to operate.

Despite the extension of *social services*, improvement of service delivery remained urgent. According to recent Afrobarometer data, most Nigériens regarded the government's performance in power generation, water delivery and sanitation as bad or very bad. The government performed better in basic health care and primary education. *Child marriage* continued to be a problem. In May, a 63-year-old man was given a four-year prison sentence and fined for taking a young girl as his so-called 'fifth wife', an illegitimate form of concubinage that dated back to Tuareg masters selling the off-spring of their slaves. The money from the fine went to the anti-slavery NGO Timidria, which had taken up the case.

Niger in 2015

The capital Niamey was struck by religiously inspired violence. Riots started in the central-eastern cities of Zinder and Maradi in protest against a cartoon of the Prophet Muhammad in the French magazine 'Charlie Hebdo' after Islamist gunmen killed cartoonists in Paris. Christian churches, bars and other establishments owned by non-Muslims were the targets of attack. Not necessarily related to this, the war against Boko Haram in the south-east began in earnest, marked by a spate of attacks, killings and counter-guerrilla operations. The flow of refugees and IDPs grew to record levels, leading to a serious humanitarian crisis in the south-east. Tension between the government and opposition mounted ahead of the 2016 presidential and legislative polls. The main opposition candidate for the presidency, Hama Amadou, who had fled to France in 2014 after being charged with involvement in a baby-trafficking scandal, returned to Niger in November to prepare for his campaign. He was immediately detained. With political temperatures rising and the country facing mounting security threats, media freedom came under pressure. The rough evacuation of civilians from Boko Haram operation zones worsened the picture. Towards year's end high-ranking army officers were arrested, accused of plotting to overthrow the government. Food security was precarious owing to the previous year's poor harvests and compounded in the south-east by the Boko Haram crisis. GDP growth declined because of depressed uranium and oil prices.

Domestic Politics

On 16 January, rioters in Niger's second city, Zinder, protested against the 'Charlie Hebdo' cartoons by pillaging churches and burning down the French cultural centre. In the ensuing violence, 45 people were wounded and five were killed. Local Christians (often West African immigrants) found shelter in a military barracks and Protestant church. The *religiously inspired violence* showed that government scrutiny of imams had not prevented the emergence of jihadi Salafi beliefs: on 17 July, the violence spread to Maradi, a city traditionally affected by religious developments in Northern Nigeria. In Zinder, however, economic competition between Christians and Muslims may also have played a role, in addition to the city's historical rivalry with the capital, Niamey. Political connotations became obvious through attacks on the offices of the ruling 'Parti Nigérien pour la Démocratie et le Socialisme' (PNDS) (including those in northern Agadez), while the violence erupted in the wake of President Mahamadou Issoufou's march with world leaders in Paris on 11 January to protest against the 'Charlie Hebdo' killings. In Niamey on 17 January, protesters shouting slogans against 'Charlie Hebdo' and France were dispersed by tear gas. This led to large groups of rioters spreading across the capital, destroying dozens of churches, hotels, drinking establishments, an orphanage and a Christian school, and companies owned by French people or West African immigrants. Security forces managed to protect Niamey's Catholic cathedral, but five people were killed and more than 120 were injured. The government declared three days of national mourning.

Although President Issoufou emphasised that he had participated in the Paris march to protest against terrorism while in no way approving of 'Charlie Hebdo', the damage had been done. The *riots' political significance* became clearer on 18 January. The coalition of opposition parties, the 'Alliance pour la Réconciliation, la Démocratie et la République' (ARDR), refused to cancel a meeting already scheduled to protest against the government's record but now the authorities (Ministry of the Interior) banned the meeting. Ninety people were arrested, among them several opposition representatives. The leader of the 'Convention Démocratique et Sociale', Mahamane Ousmane, accused the president of using the opposition as scapegoat to divert attention from his own mistakes. Thus,

Issoufou's aspiration to play a more visible role in the international fight against terrorism may have led him to underestimate the fallout of participating in the Paris march. However, frustrations over the effectiveness of Issoufou's divide-and-rule tactics also encouraged opposition forces to take more to the streets and use antisystem rhetoric.

With the 2016 elections looming, *political tension worsened.* The main opposition, the 'Mouvement National pour la Société de Développement' (MNSD) of Seini Oumarou, and the third party in the country, the 'Mouvement Démocratique Nigérien' (Moden-Lumana) led by Hama Amadou, risked implosion. In January, Interior Minister Hassoumi Massaoudou validated one of two rival MNSD congresses, which had been held the previous November. His decision played into the hands of MNSD Secretary-General Albadé Abouba, who also held the post of presidential adviser. After the January riots, the opposition ended its dialogue with the government, while the administration accused the opposition of prior knowledge of the violence. On 6 June, thousands of youths took to the streets of Niamey and called for the fall of the government. Political debate was extremely bitter, although this in itself indicated the vibrancy of Niger's political culture. However, on 19 August, NGO platform 'Alternative Espace Citoyen' called on all major political actors to engage in dialogue. In September, the UN expressed concern about the political climate. On 17 August, 30 parties, unions and civil society groups established a joint opposition alliance, the 'Front Patriotique Républicain'. It accused the Constitutional Court of presidential bias, calling for its dissolution. In its legally required review of presidential candidates, the Court had published negative statements about several opposition contenders.

Electoral procedures became an arena for altercations between the opposition and the government. On 4 June, a three-week registration process for the electoral register began. On 1 November, after rumours of lost registration records circulated in the media, thousands of people joined a march in Niamey to call for the exercise to be repeated. The electoral calendar fixed by the independent Electoral Commission (whose composition was contested) was also criticised. On 30 July, the first round of the presidential polls was scheduled to take place on 21 February 2016, simultaneously with the legislative elections. The presidential run-off (if necessary) was scheduled for 20 March 2016. Municipal elections were set to take place on 9 May 2016 – a change from previous practice when municipal elections were held before the national elections. While government and opposition agreed on 12 December on an audit of the electoral register, the latter withdrew from the exercise three days later. The threat of an opposition boycott hung in the air and the government accused the opposition of bad faith.

President Issoufou praised his *government record* extensively. He boasted of his efforts in the field of education and claimed that he had succeeded with his agricultural improvement programme. Infrastructural prestige projects such as the start of construction of the Niamey-Parakou railway were seen as electoral vote winners. On 25 February, Issoufou appointed Foreign Minister Mohamed Bazoum as minister of state at the Presidency to oversee his re-election campaign. Bazoum was succeeded at the Foreign Ministry by Aïchatou Kané Boulama, governor of the Niamey region.

On 7 November, the PNDS announced Issoufou's candidature. Hama Amadou was nominated for Moden-Lumana on 13 September at a conference in Zinder, but when he returned from France on 14 November he was detained over a 2014 baby-trafficking scandal. This did not stop Amadou, the political tycoon and kingmaker (of Mahamadou Issoufou, among others) from continuing to exercise influence. Amadou won one legal battle when on 30 January a court in Niamey threw out the charges against those involved in the baby-trafficking case on the grounds that the parentage of the children concerned was unclear. Amadou maintained that the case was politically motivated. In July, an appeals court reversed the previous judgment, deciding that the case could go to trial. Towards the end of the year, Amadou was denied bail on procedural grounds.

The administration's efforts to hinder Issoufou's *presidential rivals* by any means, including incongruous efforts that betrayed the authoritarian reflexes of Nigérien politics, provoked the opposition's anger. On 7 November, the supporters of CDS leader Mahamane Ousmane fought police in Zinder to protest against the banning of a CDS congress that was planning to nominate Ousmane as its presidential candidate. Like the MNSD, the CDS split into pro- and antigovernment wings. Ousmane was confronted with a rival for the CDS candidacy, Abdou Labo, who was close to the government but ironically also tainted by the baby-trafficking scandal. While much of this infighting took place by way of court action (a testimony to the judiciary's relative independence), Ousmane launched his own party towards the end of the year to safeguard his presidential bid. Former minister Amadou Boubacar Cissé withdrew his party from the presidential coalition and announced his own candidacy at the end of October. The government retaliated by questioning him when he submitted the paperwork required for his candidacy. MNSD chair Seini Oumarou only had his candidacy secured when the appeals court of Niamey confirmed the legitimacy of his leadership and had the faction of Secretary-General Albadé Abouba expelled – Abouba set up his own movement.

All these developments left the opposition heavily fragmented, which made an Issoufou victory likely. On 13–14 December, the PNDS headquarters were struck by gunfire. The PNDS blamed the attack on the opposition ARDR. However, in the wake of this attack the administration arrested several high-ranking military officers, accusing them of a *coup attempt*. Most details on this had not become known by year's end.

The government's authoritarian reflexes were especially felt by representatives of civil society and the media. On 18 May, the director of 'Alternative Espace Citoyen', Moussa Tchangari, was arrested on charges of having links with Boko Haram. Tchangari had criticised the evacuation of residents of the Lake Chad region in the wake of an attack by insurgents, leaving thousands of people without support or shelter. On 27 May, Tchangari was released but the charges of endangering national security were maintained. Around this time, another activist, Nouhou Arzika, was also detained on similar charges (having revealed that soldiers were complaining of a lack of equipment in the struggle against Boko Haram). The state *human rights* commission denounced what it presented as a wave of arbitrary detentions in the context of the war against Boko Haram, claiming that some individuals had been tortured. The government played down the issue but circles around the president admitted that Interior Minister Hassoumi Massaoudou had played things rough. Overall, Niger still scored fairly well in terms of civil liberties, reflecting the vibrancy of its civil society.

The *Boko Haram war* began in earnest. On 3 January, insurgents staged a bloody attack on the Nigerian town of Baga on Lake Chad (the last stronghold of the Nigerian army in the state of Borno). Chadian and Nigérien army troops, which had helped defend the town, withdrew, dissatisfied with Nigeria's military commitment. However, in a video message Boko Haram also threatened Niger and in a renewed offensive its forces began to encroach on the country's borders. Numerous young Nigériens had recently been recruited to the movement's ranks, attracted by the promise of financial gain. The authorities mobilised thousands of soldiers, gendarmes and intelligence operatives to reinforce security. On 6 February, Boko Haram attacked the town of Bosso on Lake Chad, leading to fierce fighting with Niger's military, who reported more than 100 insurgents killed. A few days later a *suicide attack* took place in the market of the provincial capital Diffa, causing at least six deaths and numerous injuries; that same day, Boko Haram fighters attacked the convoy of Niger's defence minister. On 9 February, insurgents attacked Diffa prison. Government forces repelled the assault. That same day the National Assembly approved the dispatch of troops back into Nigeria and the next day, a two-week state of emergency was imposed.

As Chadian forces came to the rescue, thousands of civilians began to leave the Diffa region for Zinder. On 17 February, unidentified fighter planes appeared over the village of Abadam, which straddles the border with Nigeria. One dropped bombs on the Nigérien side of the village, hitting a funeral procession and *killing 37 mourners*. Nigeria denied responsibility and Chad declined to comment; both countries had jet fighters active in the region (locals claimed to have seen Nigerian colours on the planes). On 18 February, the Nigérien army clashed with Boko Haram on an island in Lake Chad; 23 people were reported dead. At least 19 civilians were killed in an attack on three islands on 1 March, with many victims burnt alive. By then the authorities had reported 24 casualties among police and the military besides more than 500 on the side of Boko Haram, with another 200 of its fighters detained. This was partly the result of the Nigerian army's renewed efforts to win back territory. On 8 March, Niger and Chad launched major air and ground strikes inside Nigeria. Their troops recaptured the village of Damasak and nearby Malam Fatori, seizing large quantities of weapons and detaining dozens of insurgents. Between 200 and 300 Boko Haram fighters were reported killed, in addition to 19 Chadian soldiers and five Nigériens. Independent verification was impossible. With Chadian forces redirecting operations towards Cameroon, Boko Haram attempted to infiltrate back into Niger near Bosso on 30 March. Their forces were pushed back by Nigérien and Chadian troops. Locals spoke of intense aerial operations.

On 25 April, Niger's army suffered its *worst losses* when insurgents attacked a poorly equipped military post on Karamga, an isolated island in Lake Chad: 74 people were killed including 46 military personnel, and more than 30 soldiers went missing, while 156 insurgents, who came to Karamga in motorised canoes, were reported killed. The government ordered the population on the islands (more than 25,000 people) to leave for the mainland, abandoning them to their fate in makeshift camps. On 13 May, village chiefs who remained behind were arrested and accused of lack of cooperation with the authorities. Towards the end of May, the state of emergency in the Diffa region was extended for a further three months. This included a ban on the use of motorbikes (a favourite means of transport for Boko Haram), while women were prohibited from wearing burqas, which were used by suicide bombers.

Later in June, Chad's air force carried out attacks on Nigérien territory in retaliation for Boko Haram bombings in its capital N'Djaména. On 24 June, the Nigérien government reported that it had killed 15 insurgents and captured 20 while destroying motorbikes and an armoured vehicle. The operation came in the wake of a Boko Haram attack near Gueskérou, which led to the death of 38 civilians, including several women and children. On 11 July, *insurgents packed with explosives* again attacked Diffa prison and, on the 15th, in the wake of a Chadian-Nigérien troop withdrawal from the Nigerian town of Damasak, insurgents killed 15 villagers near Bosso, after which the Nigérien military pursued and killed some 30 attackers and destroyed numerous motorbikes. In an attack on the village of Dagaya, militants slit the throats of five civilians. August saw a relative lull in the fighting.

By September, the authorities were reporting that more than 1,000 suspected militants had been detained, but 6,000 villagers fled after an attack on Ngourtoua at the end of the month. On 1 October, insurgents killed two government soldiers near the border village of Baroua; in the ensuing fighting, which lasted five hours, an army vehicle was destroyed. On 4 October, two suicide attacks on a military camp and mosque in Diffa left five civilians, one policeman and the four insurgents dead. On 20 October, two soldiers were killed in a suicide attack on Boulongori, near Diffa. Four insurgents were killed and a number detained after an entire night of fighting. Despite the imposition of a new two-week state of emergency on 14 October, another attack took place on 27 October on the village of Ala, where militants killed 13 people and wounded three. Vehicles, houses and shops were burnt. In a major *counter-insurgency operation* in early November, army troops arrested 20 militants after a soldier had been killed by a remotely-controlled bomb near Lake Chad. On 11 November, some 25 civilians were killed in an attack on a village in the Bosso district; 20 militants were reported killed by the military.

The hostilities, unprecedented in the region, led to a *severe humanitarian crisis*. With some 100,000 Nigerians present in the Diffa region, pressure on food supplies increased. The government issued an appeal for international relief, while UNHCR set up camps to cope with the influx. In the course of the February hostilities, 50,000 IDPs made their way to Zinder. In June, the EU announced that it would provide € 21 m in aid to more than 1.7 m people in the Diffa region. By November, 200,000 people, a third of the region's population, had become displaced. WFP hoped to be able to distribute food to over 120,000 people in the course of the year.

Foreign Affairs

Niger's foreign policy agenda was dominated by the fight against Islamist terrorism – in both the Saharan region and the Lake Chad area. As a consequence, the traditional ties with *France* remained good. President Hollande visited Niamey on 18 July in the course of a West African tour. While he called on African leaders to respect constitutional term limits, France remained reluctant to criticise the authoritarian reflexes of Niger's government. When President Issoufou met his French colleague at a breakfast meeting in Paris on 2 June, they focused on the situation in Libya and Mali and the war against Boko Haram. Relations with the *United States* were driven by similar dynamics. Deputy Secretary of State Antony Blinken visited Niamey on 9 July. In October the Americans donated two military aircraft and some 30 military vehicles to improve border surveillance.

Relations with *Chad* were marked by close cooperation in the struggle against Boko Haram, while ties with *Nigeria* improved following the arrival of Muhammadu Buhari in power on 29 May. As a northerner, Buhari appeared to be committed to ending the insurgency. Following his inauguration, Buhari visited the capitals of neighbouring countries for talks and came to Niamey on 3–4 June.

On 20 January, Niger received delegates from some 20 countries to discuss the establishment of a multinational military force. On 9 February, the AU facilitated a meeting in the Cameroonian capital Yaoundé to encourage the formation of a regional force projected to number 8,700 troops. The CBLT-inspired taskforce was now set to start at the end of March. Two weeks earlier, the chiefs of defence staff of Niger, Nigeria and Chad had met for talks in Abuja (Nigeria) and decided to establish a Joint Operations Headquarters. Follow-up talks in Abuja on 9–11 June, which were also attended by Cameroon and Benin, ended in formal agreement to establish what was called the Multi-National Joint Task Force (MNJTF). The MNJTF would replace the current ad hoc arrangement and would be led by a Nigerian, with a Cameroonian as second-in-command; headquarters were projected to be in N'Djaména.

Socioeconomic Developments

Growth was expected to fall to 4.3% as a result of the poor 2014 harvest and declining oil and uranium prices. The *budget* came under pressure from rising expenditure on defence and increased spending related to the 2016 elections. On 25 May, the National Assembly increased expenditure to CFAfr 732.4 bn. Some 60% of spending was earmarked for public investment projects (which carried electoral significance for President Issoufou).

The *rains* started late but led to floods that affected at least 20,000 people; more than 2,000 homes were destroyed. *Cereal harvests* were mixed, with an overall deficiency expected to lead to food insecurity for at least 2.8 m people (15.7% of the population), particularly in the war-torn south-east.

French *uranium* conglomerate Areva announced that it had suffered a total of € 4.8 bn in losses in 2014. Difficulties with projects in other parts of the world and depressed uranium prices were to blame. As a result, it was decided to discontinue development of the huge mine of Imouraren. Only 40 of the 225 people employed at the site would be retained. In another development, workers at Areva's Somaïr mine in Arlit staged a strike on 7–9 April in protest against the non-payment of bonuses earned in 2014. The other northern city, Agadez, benefited increasingly from *illegal migration*. Many West Africans en route to North Africa stayed temporarily in the town, whose income from tourism had plummeted in recent years as a result of growing insecurity. On 11 May, the National Assembly criminalised human trafficking, to which police and customs officials habitually turn a blind eye in exchange for bribes.

Oil production at the refinery in Zinder was hindered by labour disputes, mechanical failures and arguments with the state petroleum company SONIDEP over price controls. Cheap black market oil imports from Nigeria also undermined Niger's production for the domestic market. The production of *butane gas* increased, stimulated by government consumer subsidies in efforts to fight deforestation. Production now reached 44,000 tonnes a year. Wooded areas in the south of the country had been reduced by a third in the previous 25 years. Funding for the open-cast *coal* mine and power plant in the Tahoua region was completed; it would help reduce dependence on power imports from Nigeria.

China signed two accords with Niger on 26 August involving grants and loans worth CFAfr 13.5 bn and CFAfr 9 bn, respectively. This should, amongst other things, allow Chinese construction of a third bridge in Niamey across the River Niger. China was now Niger's principal trading partner, ahead of France. Chinese investments totalled some \$ 4.7 bn and Niger boasted some 30 Chinese companies, providing employment to some 6,000 people.

In mid-August, the conventions for the construction of the Niamey-Parakou railway were signed with French conglomerate Bolloré, which would finance the costs in return for 40% of the shares in the operating company, BENI Rail (the states of Niger and

Benin would take 10% each, the rest going to private investors from both countries). The railway would link the capital with the port of Cotonou in Benin and would be used primarily for freight. In the course of the year, construction on the long-awaited project began.

A meningitis *epidemic* struck in seven of the eight regions. The west, including the capital, was particularly affected. The vaccination campaign was hindered by shortages (over half of the 1.2 m doses required were available) and by the fact that the outbreak, not uncommon in Niger, involved a rare strain of the disease. By May, the government had recorded more than 6,600 cases, with a death toll of 443.

Niger in 2016

President Mahamadou Issoufou and his ruling 'Parti Nigérien pour la Démocratie et le Socialisme' (PNDS) consolidated their grip on power, though not without pushing to absurd levels the unorthodox measures by which they hoped to strengthen their position. Opposition leader Hama Amadou of the 'Mouvement Démocratique Nigérien' (Moden-Lumana), who had been arrested in 2015 for alleged involvement in a baby-trafficking scandal, remained in detention. He was allowed to contest the 2016 presidential elections from his cell. Issoufou emerged victorious, though not without an unexpected run-off. The parliamentary polls allowed the PNDS to boost its position in the National Assembly. Although the elections took place in an atmosphere of calm, they were marred by authoritarian interventions, including the arrest of several members of the opposition. The 'Mouvement National pour la Société de Développement' (MNSD) of Seini Oumarou had to cede its leadership of the opposition to Amadou's Moden, which ended ahead of the MNSD in the Assembly. In August, the MNSD joined the presidential majority, which did not bode well for the possibility of political alternation in the future. National security was tested by frequent attacks by Boko Haram fighters in the south-east and raids by insurgents based in Mali. While the humanitarian situation in the south-east worsened, the army managed to strike back and engage in counter-insurgency operations together with forces from Chad, Nigeria and Cameroon. Overall, the country held its own, despite being sandwiched between security challenges that caused some serious losses. Rains were deficient, leading to a cereal deficit that would mean earlier shortfalls in 2017. Economic performance was affected by depressed oil and uranium prices.

© KONINKLIJKE BRILL NV, LEIDEN, 2019 | DOI:10.1163/9789004401440_010

Domestic Politics

Presidential elections were scheduled for 21 February, together with legislative polls, and a presidential run-off would take place, if necessary, on 20 March. All the tycoons on Niger's political scene entered the fray, joined by various lesser presidential hopefuls. These last included Mahamane Ousmane, who was strong in the eastern city of Zinder but was handicapped by a new party vehicle, and Ibrahim Yacouba, an adviser to President Issoufou, who had been expelled from the PNDS the previous year over an internal dispute. Seini Oumarou and Hama Amadou continued to be the president's main rivals. Oumarou, leading Niger's second party and with his fief in western Tillabéri, hoped to profit from the incarceration of Amadou, who was also from the west (Issoufou being from the central Tahoua region). However, while Amadou's detention was expected to hinder his visibility to voters, his party exploited it by playing the martyrdom card.

Faced with this splintered field, the opposition parties decided to rally behind a single candidate if elections went to a run-off. The effect of this deal, referred to as the 'Coalition pour l'alternance 2016' (Copa 2016), was to allow Issoufou a lead in the first round. The ruling party hoped to transform its incumbency into a 'knock-out' (by taking more than 50% of the votes in the first round), making a second round unnecessary. Issoufou's *campaign arguments* made much of the limited gains in agriculture and infrastructural development. Critics pointed out, not without reason, that the development programme had suffered from increases in defence spending and that the government had used threats to national security as an excuse to harass civil society activists and the opposition.

These accusations centred round *Hama Amadou's treatment*. While the facts of his involvement in the baby-trafficking affair remained unclear, the handling of the case had electoral consequences if not political connotations. Detained in Filingué, 180 km north of the capital Niamey, Amadou had been refused bail in December 2015. This decision was confirmed on appeal on 11 January. A few days earlier, the Constitutional Court had validated his presidential candidature. On 9 February, however, it declared itself incompetent to decide on Amadou's provisional release. This led to a situation in which a principal opposition leader was allowed to contest presidential elections while being kept in detention, barred access to the media and hindered from receiving visitors. Issoufou's administration hid behind the judiciary's independence. The governor of Filingué prison, however, was allegedly transferred after allowing Amadou an opposition visit on 25 January that sealed the Copa alliance.

The run-up to the elections was marred by the government's *authoritarian interventions*, thinly veiled by references to national security. By March, several of Moden's staff were behind bars on charges that varied from creating a disturbance at Niamey airport at the time of Amadou's home-coming in November 2015 to involvement in a ten-year-old corruption case and collusion in the alleged coup attempt in December 2015. Interior Minister Hassoumi Massaoudou (PNDS secretary-general and an Issoufou hardliner), together with Mohamed Bazoum, minister of state at the presidency and campaign manager, accused the opposition of complicity in the putsch. One presidential contender was briefly detained for casting doubt on the reality of the coup. Seven Moden leaders were convicted in July (for the airport disturbance) and released upon completion of their sentence in September. In early February, a Moden-loyal griot who predicted the president's electoral defeat was taken into custody for defamation (griots are used in 'séances de tam tam', political events accompanied by dance and song). Although a court in Niamey freed her on 15 February for lack of evidence, indicating the judiciary's relative independence, this could not conceal the government's reliance on unorthodox tactics. A Moden rally held in Dosso on 2 February was followed by clashes between Amadou supporters and police in Niamey the following day.

Electoral procedures were scrutinised, leading to the removal from the register of 25,000 duplicate names and the elimination of hundreds of 'ghost' polling stations. The exercise was approved by

OIF observers. However, on 17 February the Council of State decided to allow 'voting by witness' for those without identity documents (i.e. by allowing a witness to vouch for them – a common occurrence in a poor country like Niger, and such voting had been allowed before). Opposition forces cried foul, arguing that this would open the sluice gates to fraud.

With a reported turnout of 66.8% (rather high by Nigérien standards), the biggest surprise was Issoufou's failure to achieve a knockout. His support stood at 48.4%, falling short of 50% by 167,000 votes, although he took 12% more than in the 2011 polls and came in ahead of other candidates in six out of eight regions. The interior minister expressed disappointment and admitted that Amadou's detention had helped the Moden leader. The results showed *Amadou's resilience.* He received 17.8% of the votes, taking the lead in the regions of Niamey and Tillabéri. This meant that he had beaten Seini Oumarou, formerly Niger's number 2, who took 12.1%. The leader of the MNSD, which had fractured under government pressure in 2015, lost 11% compared with 2011, most of these votes going to Issoufou, who made inroads in MNSD strongholds in the Maradi and Diffa regions. Of the weaker candidates, Mahamane Ousmane took 6.3%, indicating the final eclipse of the influence of the former National Assembly chair. Surprisingly, Ibrahim Yacouba, who had broken with the PNDS, took 4.4% of the votes. In the legislative elections, the PNDS won 75 of the 171 seats in an Assembly expanded from 113 seats in 2011. With the smaller parties in the presidential coalition, it secured 112 seats. Moden-Lumana became the second party with 25.

Opposition leaders renewed their call for Amadou's release at Niamey's appeals court, but a verdict was not expected before 28 March, eight days after the run-off. As it was clear that Copa 2016 could never attract more than 40% of the votes, *divisions in the alliance* quickly manifested themselves. The PNDS curried favour with the 'petits candidats'. Ibrahim Yacouba was seen as the key to an Issoufou victory and was won over to the presidential side. On 8 March, Copa called for a boycott of the second round, but as Amadou himself decided to maintain his candidature this was to be partially ignored by voters. In the midst of this confusion, Amadou was hospitalised on 11 and 14–15 March, suffering from exhaustion and eye problems. Prime Minister Brigi Rafini dispatched a medical team, but on 16 March – four days before the run-off – the political tycoon was brought by helicopter to Niamey and flown to France for treatment.

The Electoral Commission reported a turnout of 59.8% in the *run-off*. While the EU and OIF noted the drop in participation, the opposition claimed the figure was closer to 10%-11%. If this was too low, the turnout reported by the Commission seemed high (its website listed turnouts in nomadic regions close to or surpassing 100%). In the run-off, Amadou took 7.5% of the votes, which in the circumstances was an achievement. Issoufou's 92.5% was judged by opposition voices to be of 'Stalinist' proportions. The damage to the political system was illustrated when Copa rejected the result, flatly denying that Issoufou had been re-elected. It rebuffed an invitation to form a government of national unity. To make matters worse, the Supreme Court ruled three days after the polls that civil proceedings on the parentage of the children in the trafficking scandal should be pursued before a criminal prosecution. Consequently, on 29 March, Niamey's appeals court granted bail to Amadou, who stayed in Paris, still under formal suspicion. The procedural logic of the courts allowed opposition politicians to claim that the case had been politically motivated.

The PNDS boosted its majority in the *new cabinet*. Brigi Rafini, not part of Issoufou's inner circle but important, as a northern Tuareg, for the government's stability, was retained as prime minister. Bazoum's appointment as minister of state with a super-portfolio including interior affairs, security and religious issues confirmed his importance (as did Hassoumi Massaoudou's move to defence, a key ministry). Yacouba Ibrahim, the new rising star, became foreign minister as a reward for his support in the run-off.

More than 50 opposition politicians boycotted the Assembly's inaugural session on 24 March, when Ousseini Tinni, PNDS MP for Dosso, was elected parliamentary chair. This meant that both the presidency and the *National Assembly* were now under the control of the same party (the parliamentary chair had traditionally gone to the candidate who came third in the presidential elections). Inevitably, the reality of their defeat forced opposition forces to come back to the fold, returning to the National Assembly and rejoining the Electoral Commission, whose neutrality had become – for the first time in its history – a bone of contention. This put further pressure on Copa 2016 – a coalition of convenience – and notably on the MNSD, which had suffered irreparably through the government's tactics. On 13–14 August, it decided to join the presidential majority. This left Moden out in the cold, especially as Amadou continued in exile. On 31 August, Moden and ten minor groups decided to form a new coalition, the 'Front pour la Restauration de la Démocratie et la Défense de la République', whose strongholds were Niamey and Zinder. A meeting between Oumarou and Issoufou shortly after the MNSD's decision to join the majority was followed on 19 October by a *cabinet reshuffle*. Oumarou was appointed high representative at the presidency and MNSD lieutenants took minor ministries. In the enlarged cabinet, Hassoumi Massaoudou moved from defence to finance, whose minister was ill.

Details emerged over the alleged coup attempt at the end of 2015. Sixteen civilians were kept in detention, as well as 20 military personnel from an elite anti-terrorist unit. The unit was disbanded and its commanding officer detained, as was his deputy who had fled to Togo. The plan for a helicopter-led bombardment of the presidential palace leaked out as putschists sought counsel from marabouts and contacted members of the presidential guard. Although investigators would have spoken to Amadou about the attempt, the involvement of civilian politicians remained hazy.

The *war with Boko Haram* continued unabated. By July, there were more than 300,000 IDPs in the Diffa region. The regional economy had come to a halt, with markets closed and the trade in fish and peppers (key local products) suspended. From November 2015,

100 schools – a Boko Haram target – were moved to safer locations. On 17 March, an army commander became the victim of a suicide attack in Diffa. Around the same time, five suicide bombers, including a young girl, attacked an army detachment further east in Bosso, on the borders of Lake Chad. An army commander was killed and four Boko Haram fighters died, while the girl, who failed to detonate her explosive vest, was shot. Bosso, an exposed locality, was again a target on 19 May, when at least six civilians were killed (four burned alive). The army lost 26 men in a sustained attack on Bosso on 3–5 June. Numerous soldiers were wounded and 55 Boko Haram fighters were reported killed. The insurgents, who included what locals called 'enfants du marabout' (child soldiers, apparently drugged), managed to occupy the town for several days. The population fled (all 6,000, plus 20,000 IDPs). Some 50,000 people made their way west, swelling overstretched facilities elsewhere. Confronted by heavy artillery, army troops withdrew before Niger's two Sukhoi jet fighters and helicopters stationed in Diffa intervened.

The government speeded up a *counter-insurgency operation* planned together with Chadian forces. As part of the four-nation 'Force Multinationale Mixte' (FMM), which included Nigerian and Cameroonian troops, 3,000 Nigériens and 4,000 Chadians swept into Nigeria. On 25–28 July, they liberated Damasak, though not without heavy fighting. The Nigerian border town, on the banks of the Komadougou-Yobé River, had been in the hands of insurgents on and off for a year. Niger's long-term military objective (i.e. pushing Boko Haram towards the islands in Lake Chad and the Nigerian city of Maiduguri, where they could be trapped by FMM troops) still seemed a long way off, however. On 30 July, dozens of inhabitants of the village of Gaduraa were murdered by insurgents. Many had their throats slit. On 2 September, the village of Toumour was targeted – five people died and two were injured. The insurgents fought the village self-defence group, which was armed with bows and arrows. On 12 September, 30 insurgents and five army soldiers were killed in fighting near Toumour. In mid-September, Chadian and Nigérien forces reportedly killed 38 fighters in operations near Toumour and Gueskérou (the latter had been attacked on the night of 14 September, with huts burnt and food supplies looted).

By 30 September, the civilian body count since 6 February 2015 had risen to 177. Nevertheless, Boko Haram appeared to have been dealt a blow, as its attacks grew fewer. On 27 December, the authorities reported the *voluntary surrender of insurgents* – for the first time ever. Around 50 young adults from Diffa (including women) were brought to a centre where they would follow a deradicalisation programme. Many of them hailed from Diffa and had been lured by insurgents with promises of up to $ 500 a month (a fortune by local standards). They would benefit from an amnesty and programmes destined to achieve their socioeconomic reintegration.

Attacks from Mali were a reminder of the country's vulnerability to security threats from the Saharan region. On 17 March, three gendarmes were killed near the Burkinabè frontier by men said to belong to al-Qaeda-in-the-Islamic-Maghreb (AQIM). On 28 April, one gendarme was killed and two wounded in an attack in the Azaouagh region near the border with Mali. The attackers were said to belong to the 'Mouvement pour l'Unicité et le Jihad en Afrique de l'Ouest' (MUJAO) or another Islamist group, Ansar Dine. Later, on 11 September, unidentified men killed two civilians in a UN-run refugee camp in the north-west. Much worse was an attack by 30–40 heavily armed assailants on a camp in the Azaouagh on 6 October. Twenty-two men charged with the camp's protection died. In response, Niger, together with UN and French forces, launched an operation in Mali's Ménaka region. On 14 October, an American missionary in Abalak (between Tahoua and Agadez) was kidnapped, possibly by men belonging to MUJAO. Two guards were murdered. Three days later the army repulsed an attack on the high-security prison of Koutoukalé, 50 km north-west of Niamey, which housed jihadists from Mali and the Boko Haram zone. MUJAO was said to be responsible. On 8 November, five soldiers were killed and three wounded in an attack on the border town of Bani Bangou. Two of the assailants, who arrived with vehicles and motorbikes, were killed. Several local people were arrested on suspicion of complicity.

A *Tubu leader* in the south-east issued a video message in September, announcing the establishment of a rebel 'Mouvement pour la Justice et la Réhabilitation du Niger'. Adam Tcheke Koudigan presented himself as the successor of a Tubu rebel leader in the 1990s, who died in a hospital in Dubai in July, and called for a greater portion of revenues from the oil wealth in his region to be used to benefit marginalised Tubu nomads. In unrelated violence, 18 people died in *clashes between peasants and pastoralists* in the Madaoua region on 1 November. The victims were predominantly women, children and the elderly (seven were burnt alive). The violence was triggered when a herd of cattle devastated a millet field. Hundreds of whipped-up Hausa youths armed with machetes went on the rampage in a Peul village. Local police were overwhelmed.

Foreign Affairs

Western governments remained silent over the deterioration of the political climate, as Niger was seen as a solid partner in the struggle against terrorism. *France* invited Issoufou to the Elysée on 14 June. Afterwards, he dined with Foreign Minister Ayrault. Accompanied by his foreign and defence ministers, he also met French Defence Minister Le Drian, as well as the mayor of Paris, the president of the French National Assembly and representatives of the French employers association Medef. The visit highlighted Niger's privileged ties with France.

Germany boosted its profile with a visit by Foreign Minister Steinmeier, together with his French counterpart, on 3 May. International terrorism had much to do with this, in addition to the problem of illegal migration (the northern city of Agadez being

West Africa's main migrant processing point on the route across the Sahara). Chancellor Merkel visited Niger on 10 October and promised $ 27 m in aid, to be targeted at development in Agadez and the procurement of defence equipment. The *US* announced on 30 September the establishment of a base for surveillance drones in Agadez.

Relations with African countries were also dominated by the terrorist threat. After the coming to power of Muhammadu Buhari in *Nigeria* in 2015, relations with Niger's southern neighbour had improved substantially. Nigérien troops could more easily move into Nigeria in pursuit of Boko Haram, while military cooperation also improved. The 8,700-strong FMM force still struggled with a shortage of funds, however. In response to the attacks from *Mali*, the government pleaded for a more offensive mandate for MINUSMA, the UN peacekeeping force stationed there, to which Niger was contributing 1,700 men. At a meeting of the G5 Sahel (Burkina Faso, Mali, Mauritania, Niger and Chad) on 4 March, defence ministers announced the establishment of a rapid intervention and counter-terrorism force to be deployed in areas threatened by AQIM. Technical assistance would be provided by Spain and France, which promised $ 47 m in counter-terror training. *Algeria* decided to improve surveillance of its southern borders, including with Niger, for which 20,000 military personnel would be moved south. Finally, *Libya* remained a source of concern to the government, which spoke of the 'Somalisation' of the country, pleading for renewed international intervention.

Socioeconomic Developments

Rains were deficient and erratic, leading to flooding in the Tahoua and Agadez regions. A dozen people drowned and thousands lost homes and cattle. The *cereal crop* was disappointing. WFP announced that it needed $ 21.4 m to tide over vulnerable groups. On

26 May, the World Bank approved $ 111 m in funds to help improve the agricultural sector. The project, geared at distribution and the use of drought-resistant seeds, would assist half a million people. A local company, 'Société de Transformation Alimentaire', was successful in consolidating production of high-nutrition emergency foods based on local resources.

Due to depressed commodity prices, the *growth rate* fell to an estimated 3.8%, extending the trend set in 2015. However, the IMF (which tends to give higher estimates) readjusted real GDP in 2015 upward to 3.6%. The IMF also raised estimates of growth for 2016 from 4.5% to 5.2%, counting on rebounding prices for natural resources and greater activity in the agricultural sector (but this did not yet include figures on the 2016 cereal crop). Trade with Nigeria suffered from the war with Boko Haram. The *budget* totalled $ 3 bn, slightly lower than 2015. However, the rise in defence spending, while causing imbalances in expenditure, did nothing to diminish the deficit and made the payment of salaries in the public sector increasingly problematic.

In late April, workers at the oil refinery in Zinder went on a three-day strike, disrupting *oil production*, in protest about their pay and working conditions. The refinery suffered from a dispute with the 'Société Nigérienne des Produits Pétroliers' (SONIDEP), the state petroleum company. By October 2015, SONIDEP had failed to pay for Soraz-produced fuel worth up to $ 18.8 m. In June, Soraz was given the go-ahead to export surplus oil on its own account (7,000 b/d being reserved for the domestic market). This would allow it to repay loans made by its Chinese creditors. Low oil prices, however, continued to cause difficulties. Strike action also took place on 3–5 May at the Cominak *uranium* mine in northern Arlit, where workers protested against the incomplete payment of bonuses. The French nuclear company Areva, plagued by low uranium prices and technical difficulties, stated that payment was subject to a review of 2015 results. While Areva was trying to sell its licence for the development of the huge uranium mine of Imouraren, a Canadian company was awarded a production licence for a site at Madaouela. The government also issued four other licences, one to the Canadian firm and three to African firms, reflecting expectations that the price for yellow cake would slowly recover.

The development of *infrastructure* faced various problems. The state electricity company had to reduce output after its fuel imports from Nigeria fell by two-thirds in April. All regions but one were hit. However, on 9 December, the AfDB approved € 65 m of funding for rural electrification schemes that would extend access to power to 46,000 households (with access for a further 60,000 households planned). The AfDB also gave a loan for improving Internet access; Internet coverage would increase from 15% to 30% of the population. The government confirmed the merger of the state-owned fixed-line and mobile phone companies into a new enterprise called Niger Telecom. In 2015, 36.5% of the population had a mobile phone subscription (and less than 1% a fixed-line). Construction on the Benin-Niger railway BENI Rail stalled. While the 140 km section between Niamey and Dosso was complete, a dispute with a Beninese and French company that claimed to have been granted an earlier contract, forced the French conglomerate Bolloré to halt the planned connection with Parakou and Cotonou on the West African coast. (A similar dispute erupted with a company that had signed a contract with the military government in 2011 for the production of passports.)

In the first half of June, 34 *migrants* who were trying to cross the Sahara via Algeria died of thirst near Assamakka. They had been abandoned by their trafficker and the victims included 20 children. This was not the first incident of its kind. In 2015 alone some 120,000 people had crossed Niger's northern region en route to Europe. On 7 June, the EU announced funding of up to € 60 bn to encourage private investment in West African countries, including Niger. Figures for 2015 showed that Niger was at the bottom of the HDI.

Between January and March, an outbreak of *meningitis* resulted in 61 deaths; 30% of infections were in children. (The 2015 vaccination campaign, in response to a virulent outbreak, had not yet been completed.)

On 19–25 September, university teachers and students went on strike to protest about non-payment of salaries and grant arrears. While the *education* minister blamed this on defence spending, the anti-corruption agency announced that it had found more than 2,500 ghost teachers on the government pay-roll, which had led to substantial losses in funds.

Niger in 2017

Mahamadou Issoufou continued his second term as president unopposed, exploiting his political advantages to the full. With the country squeezed between Islamist insurgencies, Issoufou remained a favourite collaborator for Western powers. His profile as interlocutor on migration and terrorism issues delivered funds to prop up budgets stretched by security spending and depressed commodity prices. Issoufou also made use of the impotence of the opposition, which had disintegrated in the wake of the 2016 elections. The price was embittered opponents, who had to leave meaningful opposition to civil society groups (relatively strong in Niger), who took to the streets, focusing discontent on the 2018 budget bill. Security threats remained substantial, notably because of the power vacuum in parts of Mali and Burkina Faso, with which the government tried to improve cooperation. Insurgent groups staged various attacks from Malian territory. In one incident casualties included four members of US special forces. The war against Boko Haram was marked by a fall in civilian casualties but could not prevent occasional attacks and kidnappings of civilians, including dozens of girls and adolescent boys from a village north-east of Diffa. Relations with France, under new President Macron, remained close, centring on security concerns. Economic growth, which had suffered from low uranium and oil prices as well as recession in Nigeria, recovered somewhat. Infrastructural improvements were impeded by budget constraints and other difficulties. Heavy rains led to the worst floods since 2012, while resulting in good harvests.

Domestic Politics

Politically, President Mahamadou Issoufou had a free hand to pursue his second-term agenda. The opposition remained marginalised

© KONINKLIJKE BRILL NV, LEIDEN, 2019 | DOI:10.1163/9789004401440_011

as the ruling 'Parti Nigérien pour la Démocratie et le Socialisme' (PNDS) dominated the National Assembly, with the presidential majority boosted further by a range of lesser parties. On 8 January, in response to an opposition-sponsored march in protest against poor living conditions the previous December, pro-government supporters staged a counter-*demonstration* in the capital Niamey. Some 20,000 people, led by Mohamed Bazoum (PNDS chair and interior and security minister), shouted slogans in support of President Issoufou.

Prime Minister Brigi Rafini undertook two minor *cabinet reshuffles*, one in April and the other in October. The first involved the appointment of Yahouza Sadissou as minister for higher education, following violent student protests; he was replaced at the Ministry of Labour by Mohamed Ben Omar. The reshuffle on 30 October concerned the replacement of Omar Tchiana, a member of a minor party, who left the Department of Transport in protest at the suspension of measures against a transport company involved in a road accident that caused 29 fatalities. He was replaced by a PNDS minister, Mahamadou Karidjo. The portfolios of industry, population and public works also changed hands.

The transport minister's departure may have pointed to the government's self-serving tendencies, and the government was also downgraded from 'hybrid' to 'authoritarian' in international rankings as a result of its repressive reflexes. However, on 2 April, Issoufou said he would not try to modify the Constitution to create the possibility of a third term. He nevertheless remained vindictive towards his principal opponent, Hama Amadou, the leader of the opposition 'Mouvement Démocratique Nigérien' (Moden-Lumana), who remained in exile avoiding prosecution for his alleged involvement in a *baby trafficking scandal*. The long-running case, which had political connotations, led to the trial on 13 February of several accused, including Amadou. Niamey's Appeals Court sentenced Amadou in absentia on 13 March to a one-year prison term for complicity in the trafficking. The same fate befell Abdou Labo, a member of the opposition 'Convention Démocratique et Sociale' (CDS), who had been defeated as a candidate in the 2016 presidential race. Although Niger has the benefit of a relatively independent judiciary, Amadou's lawyer claimed the objective was to prevent his client from standing in the 2021 elections. This bizarre case helped to poison relations with the opposition further.

As the formal opposition was largely ineffective, NGO leaders such as firebrand Nouhou Arzika and the more reasonable Moussa Tchangari filled the void. The latter organised an anti-government march in Niamey on 13 January. It proved to be the start of a series of *protest gatherings*, which exploited disappointment over the government's failure to fulfil socioeconomic promises made during Issoufou's first term. Slogans centred on corruption, bad governance, prestige infrastructure projects, higher education and the presence of foreign troops (a sensitive issue in Niger). On 18 March, thousands of people in Niamey protested against the cost of living and called for investigations into an alleged corruption scandal concerning uranium sales; 11 opposition parties took part. On 5 April, a civil society leader involved in a lawsuit over the uranium scandal received a two-week prison sentence. On 10 April, students demonstrated in several cities. Grievances centred on study conditions and grant payments. The gathering in Niamey degenerated into fighting with riot police. One student died (there were rumours of another fatality), more than 100 students and 21 policemen were injured, and hundreds of people were arrested. The university campus, situated on the more peripheral south bank of the river, was closed. However, police violence was filmed and aired on social media. On 16 April, the authorities announced the arrest of three police officers on charges of assault. They were sentenced to jail. On 10 May, a demonstration planned by civil society groups in Niamey was banned and dispersed by the authorities. An activist who protested at the last-minute banning order was put in detention three days later on charges of inciting violence.

In the second half of the year, discontent crystallised around the *2018 budget bill*, which demonstrators deemed 'anti-social' (it involved limitations on civil service salaries, a rise in power charges and the introduction of new taxes). A demonstration involving over 1,000 people on 29 October got out of hand. Groups of protesters were blocked on their way to the National Assembly, after which fighting broke out in adjacent districts. Twenty-three policemen were wounded, vehicles and a police station were burned, and the headquarters of the Election Commission was vandalised. Three protest leaders were detained; they were released on 24 November. A consumer association involved in the march was banned, while Interior Minister Bazoum accused Moden of complicity. Finance Minister Hassoumi Massaoudou defended the 2018 budget bill, arguing that it imposed taxes on the rich. Protests did not stop after the National Assembly approved the bill on 26 November, however. On the last day of the year, thousands of people marched through Niamey.

As the handling of some of these demonstrations showed, the administration occasionally succumbed to *authoritarian reflexes*. On 17 July, journalist and union leader Baba Alpha and his 70-year-old father were sentenced to two years in prison and fines for carrying false papers. Of Malian origin, they were deprived of their citizenship. 'Reporters sans Frontières' claimed the sentence was politically motivated. Earlier, on 14 May, police detained human rights activist Abdourahamane Insar. He was sentenced to six months in prison for inciting people on Facebook to revolt. He was released on 8 June. Although his case was taken up by AI, Interior Minister Bazoum claimed Insar and others had called for violence and that they were Moden activists abusing the decriminalisation of press offences. (Admittedly, not all opposition and civil society forces were necessarily democratically inclined themselves.)

Security remained on the government agenda. Issoufou said that 10% of national resources went into staving off insurgent challenges. Attacks by *Boko Haram fighters* continued in the south-east, although the previous year's counter-insurgency operations diminished the extent of the violence. On 1 January, two or three army soldiers were killed and seven wounded in an attack in Baroua, west of Lake Chad. This came after the surrender of dozens of fighters the previous week. An unconfirmed report claimed a dozen insur-

gents were killed. The exchange took place at a time when another
20–30 fighters had surrendered, which was accompanied by a presidential appeal to Boko Haram to lay down their arms. On 9 April,
however, insurgents clashed with the army near Gueskérou and 57
jihadists were reportedly killed, including one of their leaders. They
had arrived from Nigeria with motorbikes and vehicles. The rest of
the fighters, who were reported as well-trained and informed about
army positions, were pushed back over the Komadougou-Yobé, the
frontier river. The army captured vehicles, munitions and arms (including a vehicle-mounted machine gun that had been stolen in a
fierce attack on Bosso near Lake Chad the previous year). A dozen
soldiers were injured.

The assault ended the relative calm that had set in after the surrender by Nigérien Boko Haram fighters (totalling 130–150 by April).
On 28 June, two female suicide bombers set off explosives in an IDP
camp in Kabélawa (south of Nguigmi), killing two other people and
wounding a dozen. It was the first attack on such a camp on Nigérien
soil. Like the attack on Baroua, it took place further away from the
Nigerian border. On 2 July, insurgents arrived on foot in the village
of Ngaléwa (close to Kabélawa), known to be hostile to Boko Haram.
They slit the throats of nine people and adducted 37, all young girls
and boys – the first *mass kidnapping* in Niger. On 5 July, one of Niger's jet fighter planes killed 14 displaced farmers by mistake in the
village of Abadam, straddling the border with Nigeria. Having returned to tend to their fields, two Nigériens and 12 Nigerians perished in the attack; this was not the first incident of its kind, the
Nigerian army having made similar mistakes in the past. A Nigérien
journalist said that the army had been nervous about recent attacks.
During July, a further 7,000 refugees left the region, crossing into
Chad. On 21 August, the army reported having killed 40 Boko Haram
fighters, but Niger's strategic position deteriorated in October as a
result of the withdrawal of hundreds of Chadian troops in response
to fiscal problems. It was reported, moreover, that traders in the regional capital Diffa, whose businesses were suffering from a ban on
the trade in food and fuel, were compensating for their losses by

trading with the enemy. On 15 October, Diffa's governor warned that the offer of an amnesty would expire on 31 December. UN figures in August mentioned a total of 540 civilian victims in Niger so far, including those killed, wounded and abducted. Civilian fatalities had dropped, however, from 227 in 2016 to 141.

Fighting in the north-west was fiercer. On 22 February, an army patrol ran into an ambush near In Tirzawane, close to the border with Mali. A dozen or more military were killed and 19 wounded. The insurgents, allegedly of a jihadist group led by Adnane Abou Walid al-Sahraoui, formerly a member of the Polisario front, who had sworn allegiance to Islamic State, captured seven vehicles and burnt four. The assault demonstrated the striking power of the several dozen insurgents, who arrived heavily armed and equipped with motorbikes and vehicles from the Malian Ménaka region, evading French, Malian and Nigérien intelligence. In response, France announced its willingness to station counter-insurgency troops (50–80 men) to provide aerial guidance to the Nigérien military. On 6 March, three days after the declaration of a *state of emergency* in the Tillabéri and Tahoua regions, a gendarmerie post was attacked in the Gourma region, close to the borders with Mali and Burkina Faso. Five gendarmes were killed. Two French Mirage fighters stationed in Niamey intervened, as well as French helicopters from Gao (Mali). The insurgents, possibly from the 'Mouvement pour l'Unicité et le Jihad en Afrique de l'Ouest' (MUJAO), were driven off. In mid-September, the government extended the state of emergency for a further three months.

These measures could not prevent an attack near the village of Tongo Tongo on 4 October, again staged from the Ménaka region. The ambush drew publicity as the victims included four members of *US Special Forces*, one of whom appeared to have been executed. Four Nigériens died, while two Americans were injured. The American forces, present to train Nigériens in counter-insurgency operations, were 12 in total and were patrolling the border together with 30 Nigérien military. The troops were allegedly lured into extended discussions with village elders, allowing 50 fighters to lay an ambush. The insurgents, who, according to the International Crisis Group, had re-

cruited youngsters from the local Fulani community, were described
by the Americans as associated with Islamic State. Locals suggested
al-Sahraoui. The US-Nigérien operation appeared poorly prepared, as
troops were lightly armed and unaware of the risk of attack. Lacking
back-up personnel, they had to be rescued by French forces in Mali.
The US Africa Command (AFRICOM), started an inquiry whose results
were not expected before year's end. Niger's government declared
three days of mourning. A Tongo Tongo elder was arrested for complicity, and President Issoufou convened a session of the 'Conseil National de Sécurité'. Nevertheless, another attack took place on 21 October. The insurgents arrived in vehicles and were armed with rocket
launchers. They attacked a gendarmerie post at Ayorou, capturing
a large stock of weapons, ammunition and vehicles. Thirteen gendarmes were killed and another five injured. In an ominous sign of
the gradual escalation of the insurgency, the government announced
on 4 November that it would allow the US to arm its surveillance
drones. Moreover, it became clear that the American involvement in
the fighting at Tongo Tongo in October did not represent an isolated
incident, when it was confirmed early in 2018 that US Special Forces,
in conjunction with Nigérien military, had also fought militants on 6
December. Eleven jihadists, reported to be aligned to Islamic State,
were killed. US and Nigérien forces suffered no casualties.

Foreign Affairs

With Niger playing a key role in sub-regional security, relations with
France remained close. President Issoufou held separate talks with
his new French counterpart President Emmanuel Macron at the
G7 summit in Sicily on 26 May. On 2 July, the two men met at the
Bamako summit of the G5 Sahel countries (Chad, Niger, Burkina
Faso, Mali and Mauritania) and at a similar event in New York on 18
September. On 13 December, Issoufou flew to France, meeting the
French president in multilateral discussions on G5 military coopera-

tion. On 22–23 December, Issoufou welcomed Macron, his defence minister and the French chief of staff in Niamey, where the French president celebrated Christmas with the 500 French troops stationed there. The Niamey base hosted Mirage jet fighters and drones. Like the Americans, whose air facility is in Agadez, the French decided to arm their surveillance drones before 2020.

Niger also tried to improve military cooperation with *Mali and Burkina Faso*, as the faltering peace process in Mali was leading to a worsening power vacuum in the border zone. On 24 January, the three countries announced they would share intelligence and operational resources to combat insecurity in the Liptako-Gourma region, where the borders of the three countries meet and jihadists had taken refuge. The force would be modelled on the four-nation 'Force Multinationale Mixte' (FMM) of Nigérien, Chadian, Nigerian and Camerounian troops fighting Boko Haram. On 9 May, Niger signed an accord on judicial cooperation with both Mali and *Chad*, facilitating the sharing of intelligence and extradition procedures.

More broadly, Niger participated in the security cooperation of the *Sahel G5*. On 6 February, the five nations met in Mali and resolved to establish a joint force to combat terrorism and drug trafficking (a kindred decision had already been taken the previous year). Pushed by the French, it was now rumoured that the force would number 10,000 (5,000 during a first phase). The summit in Bamako (Mali) on 2 July discussed the issue of funding. With a requirement estimated at € 423 m, the G5 countries announced a joint contribution of € 10 m, while the EU pledged € 50 m and France € 8 m. Thus, while having the FMM in mind (which also had a long gestation period), the project proved financially daunting. President Issoufou proposed that the G5 force become a brigade within the UN peacekeeping mission in Mali, MINUSMA, whose € 1 bn budget could then be involved. The headquarters of the force were established in Sévaré (Mali) on 9 September and it became operational on 1 November While Morocco pledged logistical and training assistance, the financial issue continued to bedevil the project as the US remained lukewarm about integration in MINUSMA for fear of increasing UN peacekeeping costs. At discussions in France on 13 December, Saudi Arabia pledged € 100 m for the force, followed by the UAE (€ 30 m) and the Netherlands € 5 m). The US eventually pledged € 60 m.

On 3 March, members of the UNSC began a tour of the three countries hit by the Boko Haram insurgency, starting in Cameroun. The *EU* meanwhile tried to stem the outflow of migrants via the Sahara by providing Niger with a grant worth € 610 m. With Agadez the main transit point for West Africans en route to North Africa, it was hoped this money would help Niger to improve *migration* policing. The European Border and Coast Guard Agency Frontex resolved to set up a base in Agadez before year's end so that EU officials could process migrants there. In previous years, the government had set up transit centres financed by the EU and the International Organisation for Migration in Niamey, Arlit, Agadez and Dirkou to assist migrants willing to return home. While the government claimed that the number of migrants passing through had dropped by 80%, many of these now avoided Agadez and other checkpoints by navigating the more dangerous desert routes. On 17 July, the EU announced that it had released € 10 m for the Nigérien government, with a further € 10 m to follow before year's end. The amounts would be used to tackle the deeper causes of migration. At a conference in Paris on 28 August to discuss migration issues, President Issoufou and his Chadian counterpart pointed out to Western partners that, if they wished to eradicate the problem, African countries required more assistance in terms of development aid. The conference agreed to a proposal put forward by President Macron to provide Niger and Chad with official powers to register and process legal migrants to Europe.

Socioeconomic Developments

Rains were heavy, boding well for the country's cereal harvest. However, they also led to the *worst floods since 2012*. In September, it was estimated that nearly 200,000 people were affected. Fifty people died, mostly in the Niamey region, more than 12,000 ha of agricultural land was destroyed and over 15,000 head of cattle drowned. The principal regions affected were Tillabéri, Maradi, Zinder and Dosso. The government developed an assistance plan.

Economic growth improved somewhat and was estimated in November at 5.2%, but this was insufficient to keep up with population growth and could not alleviate Niger's budget difficulties either. Faced by disappointing sales to recession-struck Nigeria (which would normally absorb one-fifth of Niger's exports), the government had already cut less important expenditure in 2016. Public debt had escalated from 26% of GDP in 2012 to 48% in 2016. The 2018 budget of € 2.9 bn (a 2.5% increase) foresaw tax increases, reductions in expenditure and the scrapping of tax exemptions. The IMF applauded the measures. On 23 January, it approved a three-year ECF credit of $ 134 m, with an immediate disbursement of $ 19.2 m. An IMF mission to Niamey on 6 November deemed Niger's macroeconomic performance as generally satisfactory. According to the World Bank's 'Doing Business' index, the *business environment* had improved (Niger rose from 164th to 150th of 190 countries). This could not prevent a deterioration in the legal battle waged with *Africard*, a Lebanese-owned company that had won a contract with Salou Djibo's military government in 2011 for the production of passports. Having cancelled the € 53 m contract later, Issoufou's government vainly pleaded its case before various tribunals. Africard now proceeded with the seizure of government property in France and the US.

Construction of the *Niger-Benin railway* continued to be mired in problems similar to those with Africard. On 29 September, the Supreme Court of Benin confirmed judgements in favour of a Beninese company claiming to be the owner of the contract, to the detriment of French conglomerate Bolloré, Niger's favoured partner, which had built the railway section between Niamey and Dosso. Issoufou's government continued to refuse to deal with the Beninese company or a Chinese alternative proposed by Benin in an effort to resolve the deadlock. Without the section between Dosso and Parakou, the railway, which was intended to link Niamey with Cotonou, remained inoperative. On 2 April, President Issoufou opened a 100 MW *power plant* near Niamey. Despite the slogan 'electricity for all', the country still suffered numerous power cuts, notably in the hot months of April and May when air conditioners work around the clock. On 24 November, the AfDB agreed to provide \$ 107 m for the upgrading of the road linking Niger with Burkina Faso. Additional funding came from the EU, Japan and the Burkinabé government.

The government banned *artisanal gold mining* in two regions. In the Djado plateau in the north-east, it imposed a shutdown in February, fearing gold mining could become a source of revenue for insurgents and increase trafficking (artisanal mining had exploded since discoveries in 2014). On 15 July, a ban was imposed in the Liptako region close to Burkina Faso, where more than 20,000 people had been mining deposits for several decades. The government justified this measure with allegations of anarchy on the mine sites.

Despite efforts to curb *illegal migration* across the Sahara, the outflow of (West) Africans via Niger continued unabated. Opting for the more dangerous desert routes to avoid checkpoints (since 2015 traffickers also risked severe penalties), numerous people paid with their lives. On 21 May, 44 bodies, including of babies, were recovered near Agadez. The victims' vehicle had broken down and people had died of thirst. Only six managed to reach safety. Earlier that month, eight Nigérien migrants, including five children, died on their way to Algeria. In mid-June, the army rescued a group of 100 persons abandoned in the desert by their trafficker – a regular occurrence and one that brings a certain death sentence. On 25 June, the army rescued 24 people from a group of 70 abandoned in the Ténéré sand desert en route for Libya. The others were assumed to have perished. With the economy and population of Agadez having grown significantly from this gruesome trade, the government invested more than € 60 m in the city's infrastructural development in an effort to revamp its tourist potential. In September and October,

Algeria expelled 7,800 West Africans to the border with Niger, where they faced difficult conditions. It was estimated that some 100,000 people from SSA were living illegally in Algeria. Public opinion was shocked by reports of migrants being sold into slavery at auctions in Libya. A group of 25 from the Horn of Africa was evacuated to Niger on 11 November. Niger summoned the Libyan ambassador for talks on 19 November.

There was no let-up in terms of the deeper causes of these problems. One issue, Niger's *demographic situation*, received renewed attention, however. President Issoufou expressed an aim to bring the population growth rate down from 3.9% to 3%. The government wanted to end child marriage by making education compulsory for girls up to the age of 16. The current population growth meant that women bore an average of 7.6 children, at which rate Niger would have a population (currently around 19 m) of 25 m in 2025 and 90 m in 2050. The average age was 15. On 11 July, Minister for Population Christelle Rakiatou Jackou announced that the use of contraception showed a slight increase (from 5% in 2006 to 12%), adding that she aimed to raise the figure to 50%. There was UN assistance for a programme of family planning to attain this goal, besides legislation to provide free contraceptives. On his visit to Niger on 23 December, President Macron announced that France would provide funding to boost girls' school enrolment to reduce early marriage and pregnancies.

On 8 April, Minister of Education Daouda Marthé reported that the state had been paying € 7.3 m a year to thousands of so-called 'ghost teachers'. With 80% of teaching staff made up of contract workers, the 'Haute Autorité de Lutte contre la Corruption et Infractions Assimilées' had systematically checked schools and their payrolls (salaries for temporary staff were in the range of € 114 to € 152 a month – considerable sums in Niger).

Printed in the United States
By Bookmasters